My Life With Helen

MY LIFE WITH HELEN

The Dean of the White House Press Corps through Her Agent's Eyes

DIANE S. NINE

Rand-Smith Publishing

Ashland, VA

MY LIFE WITH HELEN: The Dean of the White House
Press Corps Through Her Agent's Eyes

Print ISBN: 978-1-950544-09-7
Digital ISBN: 978-1-950544-12-7

Registered with the Library of Congress

Rand-Smith Publishing
www.Rand-Smith.com
Ashland, VA

Printed in the USA

Contents

Dedication	*vii*
Acknowledgements	*viii*
Introduction	I
The Early Days	7
Living with Helen	15
The Ladies	28
Theatre with Helen and The Ladies	43
The Cabin	47
Mama Ayesha's	53
Entertaining, Black-Tie and White-Tie Dinners	63
Speeches	80
Books	92
Travels with Helen	103
Illness Strikes Helen	119
TV and Films	129
The HBO Documentary	138
Helen's Final Book Tour	149
No Turning Back	157
Helen's Resignation	167
Different Strokes	176
Dinnertime and Death	182
Memorial Services	186
Afterword	189
Photos	197
About the Author	218

Dedication

For my late grandmother, Me-mama. I miss her fun-loving, kind ways.

Acknowledgements

First and foremost, I'd like to thank my parents for giving me life and making my life worth living. I love you.

Second, I want to thank the following friends for their support and help with this book: Maggie Kilgore, Sue Menditto, Craig Crawford, David Blank, Pat Davenport, Kathleen Silvassy, and Dave Smitherman.

Finally, a big thank you to my publisher, Rand-Smith, without whom this book would never have seen the light of day.

Introduction

Helen Thomas was the Dean of the White House Press Corps, and she was my friend and mentor. She was my "Aunt Helen." During her adult life, I probably spent more time with Helen than anyone else.

Helen Amelia Thomas was born in Winchester, Kentucky, on August 4, 1920. She was raised in Detroit, Michigan, where she attended public schools and later graduated from Wayne State University. The year after college, Helen served as a copy girl (she used to say she was a "copy boy") for the now defunct *Washington Daily News*, and in 1943 she joined United Press (later United Press International).

For 12 years, Helen had to be at work at 5:30 a.m. to write radio news for UPI, and the early hour never really changed much throughout her life. She was paid $24 a week for this privilege. She later had several beats around the federal government, including the Department of Justice; the F.B.I.; the Department of Health, Education and Welfare (the predecessor to the Department of Health and Human Services); the FCC; the Interstate Commerce Commission; and Capitol

Hill, before she began covering President-elect John F. Kennedy in 1960.

Before JFK became president, Helen encountered the young, handsome senator at a party they were both attending. Because Helen never learned to drive, Senator Kennedy offered her a ride home. She accepted, but thought he was "boring" and "not especially attractive" at the time. Helen didn't realize she would later cover this "boring" man when he became president.

Helen went to the White House in January 1961 as a member of the UPI team headed by the late Merriman Smith and was there until May 2000. In July 2000, Helen became a columnist for the Hearst News Service after quitting UPI when it was purchased by News World Communications Inc., which publishes *The Washington Times* and was founded by the Rev. Sun Myung Moon, the leader of the Unification Church, otherwise known as the Moonies.

During the years she covered Kennedy, Helen was the first woman to close a presidential news conference with the traditional "Thank you, Mr. President." And she always wore two watches to be sure she could end the press conferences on time. Helen also revised her view of the young commander-in-chief, finding him "inspiring" as president.

A woman of many firsts, Helen served as president of the Women's National Press Club in 1959–1960, and she was the first female officer of the National Press Club after it opened its doors to women members for the first time in 90 years. In addition, Helen became the first woman officer of the White House Correspondents Association in its 50 years of existence and served as its first female president in 1975–1976. Helen also became the first woman member of the exclusive journalists' club, the Gridiron, in its history, and in 1993 she became the first woman to be elected its president.

Helen traveled around the world several times with Presidents Nixon, Ford, Carter, Reagan, Bush, and Clinton and covered every economic summit. In February 1972, she was the only newspaperwoman to travel with President Nixon to China during his breakthrough trip.

Helen continued her pointed questioning of presidents throughout the Obama administration as a columnist for Hearst until her career-ending, unfortunate words about Jewish people.

I was Helen's agent for years, and in an era where media personalities often replace "journalism" with "celebrity," Helen always understood the importance of the story before celebrity. Known worldwide for her tough questioning of presidents, one time when I was with Helen, Al Neuharth, founder of *USA Today*, told a story about when he went to Cuba, and he met with Fidel Castro. They were comparing the "democracies" in their respective countries. Neuharth finally asked Castro what he considered the biggest difference between their democracies. Castro's reply: "I don't have to answer to Helen Thomas!"

Helen had a glorious sense of humor, was a rock-solid reporter, and worked as hard, or harder, than anybody I have ever known. Once when I asked her why she kept such a crazy schedule, she said, "I don't want to miss anything!"

Helen was also known for her ridiculous sense of punctuality. She set two or three alarm clocks every morning, so she was sure to wake up on time. If anyone ever traveled with her, they knew to expect to be at the airport three hours earlier than necessary. Or if you attended the theatre with her—she loved musicals—you "only" had to arrive an hour before the play began. And, of course, she also loved singing songs from musicals—which the Gridiron Club allowed her to perform every March at their annual white-tie dinner. She spent weeks rehearsing around family and friends whenever the opportunity presented itself.

Helen's family and friends were among the most important people in her life. She cherished her large family. She also enjoyed her group of closest friends—whom I always referred to as "The Ladies"—a group of remarkable women who met when they were young and had dinner every weekend for the rest of Helen's life. They often dined at Mama Ayesha's restaurant, Helen's home away from home. In fact, Ayesha and her family became part of Helen's family, too.

I have many fond memories of times spent with Helen and The Ladies at Helen's rather rustic cabin in the Shenandoah Valley, which was built by her late husband, Doug Cornell. I guess none of us were all that "outdoorsy" since the highlight of our trips to the cabin were always focused on eating dinner at the Inn at Little Washington, a highly rated restaurant near the cabin.

Because you couldn't drink the water at the cabin—when the water was even working—some of us would bring our toothbrushes to dinner and brush our teeth in the bathroom at the Inn! And then there were New Year's Eve celebrations with Helen and The Ladies—there were sleepovers, and we often wore matching pajamas.

Helen never forgot her roots in her hometown of Detroit where she grew up. She was never a sports fan, but she sure could get excited if the Detroit Tigers made the World Series—and she loved the hot dogs from Detroit so much that she would have people traveling from Detroit bring them to her in Washington.

In fact, Helen loved hot dogs, generally. When Helen was working on one of her many books, a journalist friend came from California to help her with the project. I received a call from the frustrated friend one day, bemoaning the fact that Helen wanted to socialize all the time—instead of working on the book. I talked to Helen, and she promised me she was going to get down to work. The next day, I received another call from Helen's friend. Apparently, Helen said they were going to one last dinner before working on the book. When asked who the dinner was with, Helen said, "The woman who runs the hot dog stand at the airport." Typical Helen. Always balancing a crazy work schedule with fun.

Helen helped a lot of people along the way—emotionally and financially. In her words, "You have to care about the poor, the sick, and the less fortunate."

Helen loved life. She loved clothes—particularly clothes with a leopard print. She loved good food—and good cognac. She loved a good political debate and the fact that she enjoyed a career at the center of politics. But most of all, she loved people.

One of the few things Helen did NOT love were cats, but she put up with my various cats over the years, even when they chose her lap over a room full of cat lovers.

One time in her older years, Helen answered some written questions for a magazine piece. One of the questions asked, "What has been your greatest accomplishment?" Helen's answer: "Staying alive." I hope that Helen's memory will stay alive for all of us.

I will convey some advice Helen gave as the commencement speaker to my own high school graduating class in 1980, because I think it sums up how she lived her life: "Each day can be an adventure. Leave the prosaic and pragmatic to others. Dream dreams of things that never were, and ask 'Why not?'" (Helen incorporated the original quote from Robert Kennedy which Ted Kennedy spoke during RFK's eulogy: "Some men see things as they are and ask why. I dream of things that never were, and ask why not?")

So, thank YOU, Helen Thomas, for enriching all our lives. I hope my memories in this book do Helen justice. I have told things as I remember them, refreshing my memory lapses through photos and documents I saved over the years. Overall, they were good times, but I have also included some of the low times. I want the reader to have a complete picture of the Helen Thomas I knew.

The Early Days

When people asked Helen Thomas how long we had known each other, she used to say, "I've known Diane since before she was born." She was right.

My grandmother, Lily Siegert, was lifelong, best friends with Helen's sister Isabelle, known as "Issy." They were roommates in nursing school, which was not always easy. Me-mama, as I called my grandma, was always looking to cause chaos and bend the rules, while Issy was an angel. She was prim and proper and (almost) always followed the rules. They were supervised by Sister Emma at Deaconess Hospital, and Sister Emma was not fond of Me-mama. The feeling was mutual. Me-mama went out of her way to violate the overly strict rules and regulations imposed on the nursing students by Sister Emma—but Issy rose to Me-mama's defense, and even took the blame at times.

One of the rules at the hospital forbade nursing students to buy, read, or own issues of the "off-color" magazine called *True Love*. Me-mama, of course, had to have those magazines. One time, Me-mama was tipped off by a classmate that Sister Emma was going to conduct a room search, looking for the prohibited magazines. She raced back to her room to get her stash—and put them under Issy's bed. Later in the day, Issy told Me-mama she had better dispose of the magazines. Me-mama told Issy she had already removed them. When Issy asked where she had put them, Me-mama said, "I put them under your bed." Issy was beside herself with worry. Me-mama assured her that nobody, including Sister Emma, would believe they were hers. Me-mama was right. Sister Emma told Me-mama, "I know the magazines were yours, but I can't prove it. I will be watching you." Issy did not say a word.

I guess all was forgiven because Issy helped Me-mama sneak out to go on dates, and that's how she met my grandfather and fell in love with him.

This unusual friendship was solidified the first Christmas that Issy and Me-mama spent together. My grandmother did not have enough money to go home for Christmas, so Issy insisted she spend the break with the Thomas family, who lived closer to the hospital. The Thomas family was not wealthy, but they were kind and generous.

The Thomas family lived on Heidelberg Street in Detroit. It was an ethnically mixed neighborhood of primarily Germans and Italians, with the Thomas parents having emigrated from the Middle East, from a part of Syria that later became a part of Lebanon. When they left their homeland, they came steerage class through Ellis Island. They moved first to Winchester, Kentucky, where they had relatives, before settling in Detroit. They had a large family with nine children: Kate, Anne, Matry, Sabe, Isabelle, Josephine, Helen,

Barbara, and Genevieve. They had another child, Tommy, who died when he was attending a movie and the roof of the theatre collapsed during a blizzard. The language spoken at home was Arabic, but the children spent a lot of time trying to "Americanize" their parents by teaching them English. Neither parent read or wrote English, but they were good to their neighbors and friends, feeding them during tough times. Their father, George, was a grocer, while their mother, Mary, was a homemaker.

Me-mama arrived at the Thomas home to find everyone in the family had made gifts for everyone else. There was even a handkerchief with crocheted lace around it as a gift for my grandmother. Me-mama cherished it her entire life: it was one of the few things my mom and my uncle were not allowed to touch when they were children.

Helen's Christmas gift to the family was to sing a dazzling rendition of the song "My Man," imitating Broadway singer Fannie Brice. Me-mama complimented her friend's younger sister and asked Helen if she wanted to be a torch singer when she grew up. Helen emphatically replied, "I am going to be a news reporter, and I am going to be the best reporter the country has ever seen!" Helen was 12 at the time. Everyone chuckled, but Helen went on to be a celebrated journalist, and Me-mama and Issy went on to be nurses and remained the closest of friends until my grandmother's death.

Helen often told me that she was hooked on journalism the first time she saw her own byline in her high school newspaper, Eastern High's *The Indian.* She said it was an "ego-swelling" event. She also enjoyed the fact that her role as a student reporter often got her excused from regular classes to cover other school activities. When Helen graduated from college, she was so determined to become a reporter in the nation's capital that she told a fib to her parents. She said she was going to Washington to visit her cousin Julia Rowady, who was working for the federal government and sharing an apartment with her sister. Instead, Helen moved in with Julia, and she stayed in Washington permanently. The three young women got along well, but there was friction occasionally—like the time Helen met a man she decided to have over for dinner. Without saying a word to her cousins, she shopped for the food, using up everyone's wartime ration stamps. Then, in an effort to have privacy after the man came over, Helen locked the door of the apartment, ignoring the knocks on the door when Julia and her sister arrived home.

Helen was persistent in her quest for a career as a journalist, especially after she was fired from her job as a hostess in a restaurant for not smiling enough. Eventually, Helen landed a position as a "copy boy" at the now defunct *Washington Daily News*.

Me-mama met my grandfather while still in nursing school, and she had my mom soon after they were married. Issy went by the room with the new babies at the hospital to see her best friend's newborn. She noticed the baby's color was off. Issy rushed to get the doctor and saved my mom's life. My whole family has always been grateful for Issy's quick thinking. By the time my mom was a teenager, she was babysitting for some of Issy and Helen's nieces and nephews.

As the years went by, the Deaconess nurses held class reunions every year. All the nurses brought their families. I loved seeing Me-mama's friends, especially Issy and her family.

My mom and I made periodic trips to Washington when I was a kid to take in the sights and see Helen. During this time, my family had been keeping an eye on Helen's career, and we marveled at how she ascended the political journalism ladder. These trips were among the highlights of my year. Helen invited us to the White House, and I got to go into the Oval Office with her for photo ops or attend the daily press briefings. In those days, none of these things were televised, so it was extra special to be able to witness history as it unfolded. I was thrilled to see whatever president was the current office holder. One time, I even got to sit in the president's chair in the Cabinet Room.

We usually ate lunch at Sans Souci, an upscale French restaurant around the corner from the White House, located at 17th Street and Pennsylvania Avenue. Helen invited various friends to join us. During the early 1970s, this is where I first met Helen's friend Abigail Van Buren, better known as the syndicated advice columnist Dear Abby. Abby was full of life, and I admired her sweet tooth. She sometimes had two or three desserts in lieu of "regular" food!

Dinners were spent eating at Helen's favorite restaurant, Mama Ayesha's Calvert Cafe (as it was known in those days), or at Helen's home in Northwest

Washington DC, where she cooked up a storm for friends and neighbors. Little did I know at the time, but most of these people would soon become my friends, too. I also continue eating at Ayesha's to this day.

I got to know Helen's husband on these trips, too. Helen married late in life, and her husband, Doug Cornell, was actually her competitor at the White House. They both worked for the "wires"—Helen was with United Press International, or UPI, and Doug was with the Associated Press, or AP. Doug's first wife had died from cancer, and according to Helen's cousin Julia, Helen would have Julia drive her by Doug's house just to get a glimpse of him outside of work, since Helen never learned to drive.

After Doug's wife died, Helen began secretly dating Doug. Things got serious, and they were engaged during the Nixon administration. They shared the good news with a few of their friends—who were not good at keeping secrets. Helen and Doug's engagement was announced by First Lady Pat Nixon with the president standing by her side at a retirement party in honor of Doug. Pat Nixon was thrilled she had "scooped" Helen on a story! Once the cat was out of the bag, Helen and Doug planned a wedding at the church on the other side of Lafayette Park, located across from the White House. The church is known as "The Church of Presidents." They married in October 1971.

However, their happiness was short-lived. Doug was considerably older than Helen, and he had just retired. I had come for a visit by myself a few years after they married. Helen and Doug picked me up from the airport in a limousine, which I thought was a real treat. Doug acted strange on the way to their condo, reading aloud the street signs. When we got to their home, Helen went in the kitchen to cook dinner. Doug and I were talking in the living room when Doug moved to the dining room table. He sat down at the set table, so I sat down, too. Doug picked up a fork, and said, "You know, I fished this out of the well the other day." I thought it was some kind of joke I didn't get, so I responded with a giggle. Then Doug began folding the napkins on the table. I wasn't sure what to make of all this.

We ate dinner, and Doug continued to make off-the-wall comments. Helen didn't seem perplexed, but I suspected something was wrong. I thought maybe Doug had been drinking earlier in the day, though he was not a particularly heavy drinker.

After dinner, I helped Helen with the dishes while Doug retired to the living room. The phone rang, and Helen asked me to answer it. I picked up the extension in the kitchen, and a familiar-sounding voice said, "This is Richard Nixon calling for Doug. May I speak to him please?" Covering the phone, I excitedly told Helen that President Nixon was calling for Doug. Helen asked me to tell the president that Doug was sleeping, and to take a message.

I later learned Doug was having "memory issues." Helen first noticed these issues when they were at a dinner where Doug was receiving an award, and when he got up to accept the award, Doug said he couldn't remember why they were there. The word "Alzheimer's" was barely on anyone's radar screen in those days, but sadly, Doug was its victim. Eventually, Helen had her sister Issy live with them to take care of Doug until his death. It was painful to watch such a brilliant reporter's decline, and it was heartbreaking for the few people who knew. When Doug was still working, he was known for his ability to dictate a story so perfectly that the copy editor had to make few corrections.

Helen chose not to share the tragic condition of her beloved husband publicly. In fact, even long after Doug was gone, Helen rarely told anyone he had died from Alzheimer's. Years later, I attended a luncheon for the Alzheimer's Association with Helen, and she was the keynote speaker. Even there, Helen did not mention her husband had suffered from the illness.

Living with Helen

My trips to visit Helen while I was in high school made me dream of working in Washington one day. I applied to be a page on Capitol Hill, but all the positions were already filled. Then I had a brainstorm. It would be even better to work in the White House. I did not tell anyone since I wanted to land the position on my own. Looking back, I should have asked Helen to help me. But instead, I wrote a letter to the White House when Jimmy Carter was president, in the hopes of securing a summer job. My high school classmates were skeptical, and bordered on laughing at me, so when I received a call from the White House, I initially thought someone was playing a prank on me. In fact, when I answered the phone, and a voice on the other end said, "I'm calling for Diane Nine from the White House," I responded with, "Who is this really?" When I was met with a deadly silence, I realized it actually was someone from the White House.

After sending transcripts from school, recommendations from teachers (who were amazed at my tenacity in pursuing this position—an unprecedented position for a high school student), writing an essay, and a background check by the Secret

Service, I secured my summer job. But there was one detail left. While my parents were excited that their daughter would be working in the White House, they were not comfortable sending their high schooler to Washington to live on her own. My mom called Helen to see if she had any suggestions for safe housing. Helen immediately insisted I live with her.

My parents and I were thrilled at the prospect, but how would we ever be able to show Helen how grateful we all felt? Because Helen would not accept any direct "rent" payments, my parents were allowed to pay her electric bill and phone bill, and they showered Helen with gifts. I tried to be helpful around her home, and I used the little bit of money I was paid by the White House to buy Helen dinner every so often.

I became a professional intern, coming back to live with Helen for more than a couple of summers and working at the White House, internships on Capitol Hill when Carter lost, an internship at CNN in the DC Bureau in its infancy, and an internship at UPI—where Helen worked—among others. I even used January Terms (short study periods when students focus intensely on an area of interest) throughout my high school and college years to intern and stay with Helen, too.

The first summer I spent in Washington, my parents came along to get me settled. Helen was on a presidential trip, but she arranged to leave me a set of keys and a welcome note in her condo. I had my own room, a second bedroom that doubled as a guest room and a home office. There was a twin-sized bed, a dresser with a couple of drawers that had been cleared out, and a closet with some space to hang my clothes, though the closet had about a dozen old-fashioned typewriters on the floor. In the back of the room, there was a desk with papers piled sky high.

I had never noticed before how white everything was in the L-shaped living room and dining room. It had white walls, white carpeting, and a white sectional couch in the living room that made a semi-circle near the large windows hung with white shades and white sheers. The room also featured a white marble coffee table and white cabinets with shelves that displayed some of Helen's presidential memorabilia. The only color in the room came from the Mexican-style painting hanging above the sofa, and two red, swivel, club chairs, later re-covered in a light blue and peach fabric.

The dining room featured a continuation of the white carpeting and walls, with one wall made up of mirrored tiles. There was a glass table with ice cream parlor-style chairs in white iron with a crystal chandelier hanging above the table. Against the mirrored wall was an off-white sideboard with doors for storage. There also was a wood dry sink with a cabinet underneath where Helen stored her alcoholic beverages.

I was suddenly worried that I would accidentally spill something, resulting in stains on all the white. However, I had another overriding concern. I had to take a bus to work every day since the subway in Washington was still being built, and there was not a stop near Helen's condo building. I had never been on a bus, other than a school bus, and I couldn't imagine how I would know when to get off. So, the big activity while my parents were in town was to ride my bus route several times until I recognized my stop! To this day, I remember it was the L-4, and I got off at 17th and K Streets and walked the rest of the way to the White House.

Living with Helen was like living in history. While my internships taught me a lot about how our federal government works, I learned so much more from her. Most importantly, I learned what it means to really care about government policies and how they can impact Americans and people throughout the world. I learned that most politicians have their hearts in the right place but sometimes still fall short. I learned the importance of questioning politicians and the policies they advocate and implement. And I learned the important role the media plays in a democratic society. One time I learned this the hard way.

During one of the summers I worked at the White House, there was trouble with the president's brother, Billy Carter. In the late '70s, Billy Carter visited Libya several times and was alleged to have received a loan from the Libyans. There were Senate hearings and allegations of influence peddling. On August 4, 1980, President Carter scheduled a press conference in the East Room of the White House.

Another intern and I were assigned to help write parts of a package of information about these allegations that would be given to elected officials on the Hill and to the media. Because it was so rushed, after we finished, we were asked to go to a room in the Old Executive Office Building (subsequently renamed the

Eisenhower Building) on the White House grounds to help collate and put the packages together. We did not see the cover to the package that said, "EMBARGOED FOR RELEASE."

It happened to be Helen's birthday, so we had planned to take her out to dinner to celebrate after we all finished at the White House for the day. Because of the press conference, we knew it was unlikely we'd make it to dinner since Helen would have to file her story afterward.

We asked Jody Powell, President Carter's press secretary, if we could go to the West Wing to bring Helen her birthday gifts. He said it would be okay, but to come back after to see if there was more to be done. On our way to Helen's booth in the West Wing (at the time, the wire services and the original TV networks worked in small booths off the Briefing Room since they were considered the most important media), the other intern grabbed two of the packages containing a set of documents on "Billy Gate" and commented, "These will make nice souvenirs of our work at the White House."

There was nobody there when we got to Helen's booth. We sat down to write a note saying, "Happy Birthday. See you at the press conference," to leave with the gifts, and we headed back to see if there was more to be done with the "Billy Gate" packets. We inadvertently left the embargoed packages sitting in Helen's work area. We did not realize our error until later.

As we were about to enter the room where all the collating was going on, a man grabbed me by my White

House pass, which I wore on a chain around my neck, and threw me against the wall. He said, "Do you know who I am?" I squinted to see his dog tag White House pass to no avail. The other intern said, "Get your hands off of her!" Letting go of me, the man said, "I am counsel to the president of the United States, and I know what you kids did. You leaked a story to Helen Thomas, and there will be a price to pay!" He turned and walked into the room.

The other intern and I ran out of the White House campus, to a pay phone around the corner next to a McDonald's (this was long before the days of cell phones) and called Helen. We told her that we thought we inadvertently had left the "Billy Gate" packages in her booth. Helen responded, "I thought it was the best birthday present, and I wondered who left them for me!" We agreed to meet at her place after the press conference to discuss our predicament. Helen's story was already filed, but she assured us everything was going to be okay. We had visions of being fired, or worse.

We chatted with Helen late that evening. She reassured us again and told us to go to work the following day. But the next day, the other intern and I received separate phone calls, directing us to come to a conference room in the White House complex—and warning us not to discuss the breach between ourselves.

I went first. The room had a long table with the man who had confronted me sitting at one end, and a White House transcriber with a machine similar to those found in courtrooms sitting near him. I was told to sit at the other end of the table. The inquisition was extremely repetitive, with the White House counsel continually asking me in a harsh tone, "Did you intentionally leak embargoed information to Helen Thomas?" Every time I was asked this, I tried to explain that it wasn't intentional, but rather inadvertent, but the lawyer continually cut me off before I could draw the distinction.

I was dismissed after an hour, and the other intern was waiting outside the door for his turn. I went back to my office and called my father (who is an attorney). Bawling, I told him what was happening. My dad had worked his way through law school as a lobbyist for Chrysler, and coincidentally, he had worked with Lloyd Cutler, who was now the head White House counsel. My father said he would try to call Mr. Cutler to tell him about the other White House attorney-staffer who had grabbed me by my White House pass.

Hours went by on what seemed like the longest day of my relatively short life. My phone rang, and Jody Powell asked if I could come by his office with the other intern at the end of the day. We were petrified, convinced we were going to lose our jobs. At the appointed hour, we waited outside Jody's office. Finally, we were invited in. He offered us cookies and Cokes, which only prolonged our agony. We declined. I kept thinking, "Just get it over with. Fire us. Line us up in front of a firing squad."

However, Jody finally said in his Georgian drawl, "You have a great friend in Helen Thomas. Reporters rarely reveal their sources, even when we know their sources. But Helen came to me and explained how she ended up filing a news story on embargoed information before the embargo was lifted. She said all of us should give y'all a break, and for me to make it up to you. So, I'd like to take you to dinner at the (Democratic) Convention when we are all in New York. Be sure to thank Helen and be more careful in the future when handling sensitive information."

We took Helen out for her birthday that night, but it also was a celebration of our good fortune. It was one of the few times I saw Helen step out of her professional role as a journalist at work, and it was the only time I knew of when she revealed a source—and I was grateful.

There were other birthday celebrations with Helen, too. One of the most memorable was a surprise party at the White House given by President Carter and the first lady. I was in on the secret, and I was torn. Helen didn't like surprises, but I didn't want to ruin it for her. I decided not to reveal what was going to take place. Instead, in the morning, I insisted that Helen needed to change clothes. I knew she would want to look her best at the party, but she rushed out the door, ignoring me, wearing a white dress that would be comfortable in the sweltering August heat. Her hair was not good, either.

Helen got her hair done once a week (unless there was a special occasion). She used to tell people how she prepared for a press conference: "I get my hair done. Friends and family don't care what you say, but they do care how you look on TV!" Helen did not seem to know how to brush her hair between salon appointments, so she often looked like she had just rolled out of bed. This was one of those days.

Helen left the White House to go to her bank across the street on Pennsylvania Ave. Then everyone jumped into motion, setting up for the party in the briefing room. In those days, there was no theatre-style seating for the reporters. The room resembled a shabby family room and was more conducive to large, standing crowds of people.

The White House press corps gathered with Jody Powell, President Jimmy Carter, and the first lady. My parents and a high school classmate were in town to host a dinner for Helen's birthday that evening, so they were included in the festivities. A huge cake was brought in, and many people had gifts. Someone had drawn an oversized caricature of Helen that served as a birthday card that everyone signed.

I was the lookout, in charge of letting everyone know when Helen was walking up the driveway to the White House. I announced in a loud voice, "Here she comes," and everyone yelled, "Surprise!" as she opened the door. Helen was sweating from her walk to and from the bank, and initially she looked a little bewildered. When she finally realized the people were gathered for her, she looked at me and said, "Did you know about this? You should have told me to get my hair done."

Nobody had thought to bring a cake knife, so the president cut the cake with a plastic knife, showing his down-to-earth side. As he cut, I passed out cake to everyone. I gave the first piece to Helen and offered the second piece to Mrs. Carter. She declined, telling me she was on a diet.

That evening at the dinner my parents hosted, Helen said, "I'm not sure I will forgive you for not telling me about the surprise party, but it WAS an honor!"

While I stayed with Helen, I got to know her housekeeper, Nellie Wigginton, who had become a part of Helen's family. Nellie was a biracial woman, and she identified with the black community. She was already on the older side by the time I knew her, and she was overly protective of "Miss Helen." Nellie kept Helen's place in order and was particularly fond of ironing clothes while she listened to her "stories"—soap operas she had followed on the radio, before they were televised. "Guiding Light" was her favorite, and she regaled me with daily updates on what took place on the program.

One time when Me-mama came for a visit, she noticed that Helen's trash bin was disgustingly filthy. Rather than attempt to wash it, we went out and bought a new, identical trash can. When Nellie noticed, she was not happy. She insisted "Miss Helen" liked the old trash bin and would not approve of the new one. Nellie kept at it, belaboring her point. Me-mama was artistic and often drew cartoons. I will never forget how she drew a panel of cartoons about the ridiculous trash can episode. When she showed it to Nellie, she burst out laughing, and said, "That looks just like me."

During the late afternoons, Helen's next-door neighbors, Knox and Myrtle, would come to Helen's place to visit with Nellie. They sat around the dining room table and drinks were served. Helen knew about this daily ritual but never said a word. In fact, on rare days when Helen made it home in time to witness this drinking, she would not only join them, but she would serve the beverages.

However, alcoholism eventually killed one of the neighbors. Helen was on a presidential trip, and I had played tennis, followed by dinner with my tennis friends. We were eating at Helen's hang-out, Ayesha's, when one of the waiters told me I had a phone call. This was long before cell phones, and Helen and I received calls at the restaurant from friends since we ate there so often.

This time the call was from another neighbor, Betty. When I picked up the phone, she asked, "Have you seen Helen's next-door neighbors, Knox and Myrtle, recently?" I told her I had not seen them and asked why she wanted to know. Betty excitedly told me she had called them. Knox told her he was diabetic, and his wife, Myrtle, had not fed him in days. Betty asked if I could bring some food from the restaurant for Knox—immediately. Betty was like the nosy neighbor peering over the fence.

I hesitated, not knowing much about diabetes. I suggested that Knox needed a doctor, and Betty told me she had already called a doctor who lived in the condo building. She ordered me to bring food and said she and the doctor would meet me in the hallway outside the elevator.

Irritated, I ordered carry-out chicken kabob from the restaurant and asked one of my tennis buddies to come with me to make the delivery. We told our other dinner companions we would be back as quickly as possible. Little did we know that we would not make it back to the restaurant that night.

We stepped off the elevator in the condo and were immediately overwhelmed by a putrid odor. Betty and the doctor were waiting for us. After a moment of assessing what the smell could be, I finally said, "If we're going to check on Knox and Myrtle, let's do it now." I knew we were going to find something horribly wrong.

We walked down the hallway, past Helen's door, and stood outside the neighbors' door. I finally rang the doorbell and knocked repeatedly. Just as we were about to give up, Knox opened the door a crack, enough for us to see that he was wearing dirty pajamas, and he looked as though he hadn't shaved for days. The smell got worse when he opened the door, and Knox seemed disoriented. The doctor said, "I don't have a good feeling about this."

I asked Knox if he knew who I was and told him we were there to help. He opened the door more widely, and then we saw Myrtle. She was sprawled out on the ground, face down in the entranceway. A white woman, her skin looked black. The smell was overwhelming. The doctor said, "I should take a pulse, but I know she has been dead a while based on the color of her skin." I told the doctor we wouldn't tell if she did not want to take a pulse. Meantime, my friend began gagging from the odor. Betty started crying, and Knox seemed to be unaware of anything.

The doctor called 911, and the paramedics and police

arrived. Myrtle's body was taken away, and Knox was taken to the hospital for evaluation. The police remained, ordering all of us to stay for questioning. My friend was still gagging from the hideous smell, so I convinced the police to allow us to wait in the lobby of the condo building.

While we were sitting in the lobby, Helen arrived home from her trip and wanted to know why we were in the lobby. When we told her about the drama, she said, "I thought I smelled something bad when I left a couple of days ago." I was living on my own by this time and had not been at Helen's place for more than a week, which spared me the growing odor.

The coroner's report said Myrtle's death was caused by choking on her own vomit when she was drunk. It turns out that Knox was in diabetic shock. With Helen's help, we located his daughter, who eventually moved him to Texas near her. Helen later regretfully commented, "Maybe all that drinking with Nellie shouldn't have happened." I told her I was sure that if they weren't drinking with Nellie, they would have been drinking elsewhere.

Helen certainly had some unusual neighbors. And some of her friends were different as well.

The Ladies

Throughout my years with Helen, I got to know her inner circle of closest friends, a group of quirky, but kind women. "The Ladies," as I dubbed them (Helen referred to them as "the girls"), met each other as young women and had dinner every weekend until Helen died. They spent holidays together and celebrated one another's birthdays. They were the true definition of friends for life. Eventually, I became a part of this special group, and more frequently than not, I joined them in their activities. Later, one of my closest friends, Sue Menditto, also became a part of The Ladies. While Helen had other friends, many of whom were household "celebrity" names, her heart and loyalty were always with these remarkable women. Because they were all single, they created their own family, helping one another cope with life's ups and downs.

The Ladies consisted of Fran Lewine, Dorothy Ohliger, Gloria Ohliger, Dorothy Newman, and, of course, Helen.

FRAN LEWINE
Frances "Fran" Lewine was a journalist who began

her career with a newspaper in New Jersey after being raised in New York City where she attended Hunter College. She joined the Associated Press Bureau (AP) in New Jersey and made her way to the White House for AP where she became Helen's competitor. Helen worked for United Press International (UPI), and in those days, the importance of the wire services cannot be understated. All the other media relied on "the wires" for their own reporting since UPI and AP supplied syndicated news to television, radio, and other print outlets. Fran eventually was appointed deputy director of public affairs for the Department of Transportation by Jimmy Carter, and when Carter lost his re-election bid, she joined CNN in its infancy as a producer and assignment editor in the Washington bureau, where she remained until her death.

My favorite story about the spirited competition between the two wire service reporters covering the White House took place on the day President John F. Kennedy was shot and killed in Dallas. Both of their bosses were on the presidential trip, so Helen and Fran decided they could have a leisurely lunch—and drink martinis. They were dining at Sans Souci, a restaurant around the corner from the White House, enjoying the French food and drinks, when the maître d' appeared at the table. He said, "I just saw something on the TV in the bar, and I think the president has been shot!"

Helen and Fran jumped up from the table and ran to the White House—leaving without paying the bill. Helen told me, "It was a very sobering moment, and when people ask me if I know where I was when JFK was killed, I know exactly where I was."

Helen was sent to Andrews Air Force Base to cover Mrs. Kennedy's arrival with her husband's body. She said she will never forget Jackie Kennedy's blood-stained clothes and her grief- stricken look. Helen's boss, Merriman Smith, won a Pulitzer for his coverage of the tragedy. "Smitty" was on the trip, and while everyone else initially thought the sound of the gunshots was a car backfiring, he discerned the difference.

But work wasn't the only area of competition between Helen and Fran. Helen was busy breaking barriers for women in journalism, and Fran almost always joined her, but she was always second to Helen's first. The only time I saw this friendly rivalry turn hurtful was when Helen had her memoir, *Front Row at The White House*, published. All the other Ladies expressed their excitement to Helen, but Fran never uttered a word of support. This bothered Helen, and she often said things to me like, "Do you think Fran has even read my book?"

I was Helen's agent, and Fran, obviously, knew that. Years before, I had graduated from law school, and after a short stint working on the Democratic Platform Committee in 1988, I opened my own agency. Shortly after Helen's memoir was out, Fran called me. She said she could write a good book, too, and asked me if I would represent her. I said I would be happy to rep the book and asked her what she intended to write about. She told me she was working on a book about Jackie

Kennedy, which seemed reasonable since Fran had covered all things Jackie at the White House and beyond. I mentioned the call to Helen, and she said Fran could do a great book on Jackie but questioned whether Fran only wanted to write the book out of jealousy. In some ways, I was grateful Fran never wrote the book since it might have put me in an awkward position between the two friends.

However, generally, Helen and Fran got along well, and shared a love for journalism and the fight for women's equality. During one of The Ladies' weekly dinners while I was in still in law school, Fran asked me about my classes. Among others, I was taking a class on women and the law. Helen and Fran couldn't hear enough about it—and Fran asked if she could attend one of the classes with me. After discussing her request with my professor, Fran came to the class. She was wearing a sweatsuit that matched her shirt and sneakers, and I thought it was great she was trying to dress like the students. She also participated in the class, telling "war stories" about women's discrimination. My professor invited her to come to the class again.

Fran had very few vices, but she loved vodka and gambling. She always had one vodka when The Ladies went out, and she nursed that drink to the point of refusing to let the waiter take the glass away when it appeared empty. She let the ice melt and continued to savor every last drop. When Fran went gambling, she would decide ahead of time on an amount of money she could afford to lose and quit after it was spent.

As is the case with most people, Fran was not without

some annoying habits, and these irritated Helen. Fran was usually the driver when The Ladies went out together. She picked everyone up from their homes, and after dinner, dropped everyone off. For years, Fran drove an older model car that someone had nicknamed "the Shlosher." I never knew why the car was called this, but the Shlosher did not have automatic locks. As a result, every time Fran parked the car, she would announce to the group exiting the vehicle, "Don't forget to lock the doors." This became a joke between Helen and the other Ladies, but they still were grateful for the rides Fran provided since the only other one in the group who knew how to drive was Dorothy Newman.

Fran took a lot of heat from Helen. She was the only Jewish woman in the group of Ladies, and Helen never held back when it came to her support of the Arab view on the various conflicts in the Middle East, something which ultimately ended Helen's career. But Fran had an ability to stay quiet when the subject came up, so major blowups at dinners were usually avoided. In fact, I cannot recall even one time when Helen and Fran had more than a minor disagreement.

The day Fran died happened to be the day before her birthday, January 19, 2008. The Ladies, my friend Sue (who was, by then, a part of The Ladies' club), and I were going to take Fran out to dinner to celebrate her special day. Helen had something to do earlier in the day, so she hired a car service. Helen was going to pick up The Ladies, and Sue and I would meet them at a restaurant in Georgetown, La Chaumiere. The "birthday girl" in the group got to pick the restaurant, and this was one of Fran's favorites.

When Sue and I walked into the restaurant, the hostess said, "You need to call Helen." My gut told me something was wrong, but I dialed Helen's cell number. Rather than even saying "Hello," Helen answered by blurting out, "Fran is dead! You girls need to come to her house now!"

Sue and I handled the police and coroner and tried to keep Helen, The Ladies, and Fran's neighbors (who had gathered when they saw the first responders) calm. They all looked stunned. Meantime, Fran's cousin arrived from out of town to celebrate with Fran the following day. When he heard the bad news, he fell to the ground, sobbing.

Helen planned a memorial service at the National Press Club, where she spoke about her good friend, Fran. She said it was one of the most difficult speeches she ever made. She had lost one of her closest friends.

THE SISTERS—DOROTHY and GLORIA OHLIGER

Dorothy Ohliger or "Dorothy O" (as The Ladies referred to her) was by far the quirkiest of the bunch. She had always dreamed of being an actress, but ended up as a secretary for United Press, later United Press International.

Dorothy's sister, Gloria Ohliger, was also a part of The Ladies. Gloria was a print journalist for women's periodicals and had worked on Capitol Hill. When she contracted Legionnaires' Disease, she retired early, and

Helen always said it was a "mystery" how she spent her time.

The Ohliger sisters were half Mexican, a fact that I only realized after years and years. They often cooked a Mexican breakfast on New Year's Day at Helen's home and at Helen's cabin. I eventually asked Helen if there was a reason why they always made a Mexican breakfast, and Helen revealed their heritage. However, the sisters never talked about their ethnicity.

No sisters could have been more different. Dorothy was animated. Gloria was reserved. Dorothy never seemed to have enough money. Gloria always seemed to have plenty. And, while Gloria was always "proper," Dorothy was usually off the wall—which made dinners with The Ladies interesting, to say the least.

The Ladies always shared everything they ordered at restaurants. This could become confusing to the waiter. Fran would share an entree with Helen, while Dorothy O would share a salad with Fran, and Gloria would share an entree with Dorothy Newman, and so on. Inevitably, the food would arrive, placed in front of the wrong people. I always thought there was something unappetizing when The Ladies shared one hot fudge sundae between them, "double dipping" with their spoons.

If there was any food left over after all this sharing, Dorothy O would scrape it onto her plate and ask for a doggy bag. When the leftovers were brought to her, she would literally clear the table of any food that wasn't nailed down, including bread or rolls from the breadbasket, and put these items in her doggy bag—or in a tote bag she brought along with this purpose in mind. Gloria would inevitably respond to these antics with a long, drawn out, "I'm weary," and yawn. The rest of us usually sat in stunned silence, except when Helen occasionally asked, "What the hell do you do with all that stale bread?"

Dorothy O was obsessed with the topic of sex, which made Gloria "weary" again. When Dorothy wasn't talking about her own health, she was discussing sex. She could move any conversation to the topic. Helen always giggled, unless Dorothy went too far. Then Helen would tell her, "Come on, Dorothy!"

The Ladies always spent New Year's Eve together, and it was a slumber party. Many years, we even wore matching pajamas. Helen and I lived in the same condo building (I knew I liked it from all those years living with Helen), so one of us would host a dinner, and after midnight, the group would split up, with half sleeping at Helen's place and half sleeping at mine. On New Year's Day, we would convene at Helen's for a Mexican brunch prepared by Dorothy O and Gloria.

One year, Helen invited some friends to join us on New Year's, so everyone was on their best behavior. Except Dorothy O. With a couple of scotches in her, Dorothy began acting out a scene from a book she had read. She got on the floor, and was gyrating her body up and down, over and over again. Finally, Helen said, "What the hell are you doing?" Dorothy replied, as though it was obvious, "I read a book where a couple had sex on top of a copy machine." Everyone in the room was silent, though there was some nervous chuckling.

All of The Ladies also used to be bewildered by Dorothy O's riding of the bus around town, usually to find just the "right" cucumber or tomato. She would regale us with long, drawn-out stories about these personal quests for the perfect vegetables. Her sister showed obvious irritation at these perplexing tales, but Dorothy O would continue with the details while adjusting her black, thick-framed glasses that everyone referred to as her "Devo" glasses, named after the '70s and '80s rock band.

Despite Dorothy O's idiosyncrasies, Gloria was attentive to her sister. When Dorothy's mind was failing her, she was moved from her efficiency condo near the Watergate office complex to a nursing home in Washington. Everyone in the group was somewhat surprised Dorothy O could afford the place given her preferred form of transportation of a bus and her habit of gathering all of the leftovers at our dinners. Gloria went to see her nearly every day in the nursing home, and she even arranged for a few The Ladies' dinners in a private room at the facility. We picked up Chinese food, and it (almost) seemed like the good old days.

Eventually, Dorothy's demands on her sister got to be too much for Gloria, so the Ohligers' half-sister moved Dorothy to a nursing home in Florida where she lived to take care of her.

The Ohliger sisters' kindness to me was always evident, even in their older years. When President Obama was inaugurated the first time, Washington overflowed with people who wanted to be a part of history. As a result, there were no hotel rooms to be found. I already had friends staying with me when some other friends wanted to come to town, but I didn't have space for them. I mentioned my predicament to Gloria. She immediately offered her sister's condo since Dorothy O was already in the nursing home.

DOROTHY NEWMAN

Dorothy Newman was raised in Montreal, Canada, and she was the only member of The Ladies without a direct connection to journalism. Dorothy was a real estate broker. She worked in "high end" properties, with a focus on commercial real estate. After President Nixon's breakthrough trip to China in 1972, American-Chinese relations were reopened, and China needed an embassy in Washington. Dorothy sold them the building that would serve as their embassy for years, something that was unheard of for a woman in those days.

The sale of the Chinese embassy put Dorothy on the map, not only in the real estate world, but also in Washington's social scene for embassy parties. Dorothy fit right in. She had grown up with money, enjoyed donning designer clothes, and had an outgoing, vivacious personality. All of this sometimes caused The Ladies to think of her as a snob, and Dorothy could give the impression that she looked down on the rest of the group, especially the Ohliger sisters. However, Dorothy was always the life of the party, and so much fun to be around that The Ladies didn't let it bother them.

When I was buying a condo, Dorothy agreed to help me. I wanted to live in the same building where I stayed with Helen. When a condo came up for sale, I called the listing agent to find out when I could look at it. When she proposed that I could see it in an hour, I said I would have to check to see if my agent, Dorothy Newman, was available. The listing agent gasped, and said, "You know Dorothy Newman? She is a legend!" When I phoned Dorothy, she said, "I am in my dressing gown, but I'll just throw on some pearls and be right over." I didn't realize Dorothy was being so literal. She arrived in a housecoat with a long strand of pearls! Apparently, she and Helen thought the same way. Helen often said, "Just throw on some pearls. They dress everything up."

Dorothy had two sons from her marriage, Blair and Ross. The "boys" were the light of her life, especially after their father passed away. Both men were accomplished, and Dorothy beamed with pride when she spoke of them.

Blair was a Harvard graduate, and he was brilliant, inventing prototypes of things in the emerging technology era. As a veteran of the early personal computer industry, Blair also was an active member of The Well, a sort of predecessor to chat rooms that had its roots in the 1960s counterculture.

By the late '80s, Dorothy was worried about Blair and told me she thought he was clinically depressed. She asked me not to share this with Helen or The Ladies. Dorothy said she offered to pay for a psychiatrist for her son, but he refused. She offered to come for a long visit (Blair was living in California), or to have Blair come to

Washington. Again, he refused. Dorothy had reason for concern.

During the summer of 1990, I received a phone call. The woman on the other end was sobbing so hard that it took me a minute to realize it was Dorothy. She had been vacationing in Italy when she got word from her other son, Ross, that his brother had killed himself. Dorothy got on the first flight back to Washington, and one of her first calls was to me. She could barely explain what happened.

Apparently, Blair had "scribbled"—meaning deleted—all of his postings on The Well. This "virtual suicide" enraged the community on The Well, and several weeks later, on June 1, 1990, Blair took his own life in the real world. He was 43 years old. Dorothy was devastated, and she asked me to let Helen and The Ladies know what happened.

I knew The Ladies would be upset, especially Helen, since she always felt others' pain in her heart. When I spoke to Helen, she broke into tears, and said, "Dorothy will never be the same. Oh, dear, God." Helen was right. I don't think Dorothy ever was the same. She and her son, Ross, made a trip to Montreal where Blair was buried every year thereafter on June 1 to commemorate the anniversary of their loved one's death. Eventually, Ross moved back to Washington from California where he was living to be near his mom.

However, Dorothy's upbeat personality served her well. Within a year, she was back to herself, at least outwardly. She was once again joining The Ladies for dinner, and we had our own adventures, too.

When I was on crutches due to an ankle injury that I sustained playing volleyball, Dorothy was always there to drive me anywhere I needed to go. On one such occasion, I had to go to the small town near Camp David for research on a business project. Dorothy jumped at the opportunity for an adventure. We arrived in Thurmont, Maryland, at lunch time and decided to dine at the Cozy Inn restaurant—home to the White House press corps when the president goes to Camp David. A newspaper was immediately delivered to our table, and we noticed none of the articles were dated, including an article on Helen. We learned the articles weren't dated because the identical, generic "news" paper was "delivered" daily. Dorothy was NOT impressed and wanted to find another "bistro"—but I convinced her to give the Cozy a try. The buffet lunch was equally unimpressive in Dorothy's mind, and her conclusion was: "Julia Child would not be thrilled."

Next, Dorothy decided we should see what Camp David looks like since we were "in the neighborhood." We drove up the winding, mountain road—eventually encountering several Secret Service agents.

Dorothy jumped out of the car, flirting with the agents: "How does a country girl like me get to see Camp David?"

"You don't," said an agent matter-of-factly.

Dorothy fluttered her eyes, "Just a little peek would be helpful."

"It would be helpful if you turned your car around and went on your way," replied the same agent. I think this is the ONLY time Dorothy wasn't able to talk her way into something!

Dorothy was always pleased that she was French Canadian, and she even mixed French expressions in with her English on occasion. This annoyed Helen so much that she eventually blew her gasket one time when the three of us were having a drink at my place. We were talking about someone when Dorothy asked us if we knew how old the person was that we were speaking about. Helen said in a snappish way, "What does it matter? Nobody knows exactly how old *you* are, Dorothy." To which Dorothy replied, "French women never tell their age." Helen raised her voice, "You are NOT French!" I changed the subject, but Helen brought the conversation up to me numerous times in the following years.

Dorothy had an annoying habit of rambling when she was telling a story, and then suddenly she would exclaim, "Point of story!" Usually there was no point to the story, and this bothered Helen. But Dorothy and Helen remained close until Dorothy's death.

In 2010, Dorothy became ill. She had skin cancer, and it ultimately took her life. Throughout the terrible ordeal, The Ladies called and visited regularly. She was a part of them. The Ladies often fought like cats and dogs, but they were true friends. After Dorothy's death, Helen summed it up, "Point of story. We will miss Dorothy."

I kept in touch with Dorothy's son, Ross, until he tragically was found dead from natural causes in a hotel room in Montreal. He was there to go to a reunion with friends who had attended his prep school with him when he was a boy.

Theatre with Helen and The Ladies

Helen and The Ladies always enjoyed seeing movies on the big screen, and it was always a memorable experience. They would shout angry, happy, or confused words at the screen throughout the film for the entire audience to hear. Helen was particularly adept at this. Her familiar voice could be heard ricocheting through the otherwise quiet theatre.

There are a couple of films we saw together that stand out. A New Year's Day tradition with The Ladies was to go to see a movie after the slumber party on New Year's Eve and a hearty brunch the following morning. One year, we went to see the film *A Room with a View*. Based on a novel by E.M. Forster, the British romantic drama had been out a while, but it was being shown at a small theatre in Washington.

The Ladies seemed to relish the romantic plot while feasting their eyes on the beautiful scenery of Italy and England. This was encouraging since they could be a hard group to please. All of a sudden, as the theatre was deathly quiet, some men in the film jumped into a pond displaying full frontal nudity. I would have barely noticed but for the uproar emanating from my row of seats with The Ladies. Helen led the commotion, shouting in an extremely loud voice, "Their penises are showing! Their penises are showing!" As I slunk down in my seat, The Ladies erupted with chatter about the men's genitalia. Other people in the audience shushed them—and I pretended I was not with them.

Another memorable film I saw with Helen and The Ladies was *Working Girl*, a romantic comedy starring Melanie Griffith, Harrison Ford, and Sigourney Weaver. I was satisfied the movie was a good choice to see with The Ladies. What could go wrong in a comedy? Little did I know.

Unfortunately for me, there are plenty of scenes in the movie of Melanie Griffith's character, Tess, in her bra and underwear, or topless. I braced myself for the inevitable onslaught of comments from The Ladies as each scene unfolded on the screen. And the comments came. However, none surpassed the comment made by Helen as Melanie Griffith's character vacuumed her apartment in her panties, topless. Helen blurted out in an overly loud voice, "Oh, come on. Who vacuums only wearing underwear?" To which all The Ladies felt it necessary to express their agreement. The running commentary interrupted other people in the audience, and we could hear lots of people saying, "Shhhh!" The attempts to quiet The Ladies were fruitless.

Another movie I saw with Helen and The Ladies that is worth recalling was Oliver Stone's film, *Nixon*. Helen was particularly anxious to see this biographical drama of former President Richard Nixon. And from the moment the movie began, she had a running commentary about perceived inaccuracies of how the characters were portrayed. Making no effort to whisper or even keep her voice down, Helen shouted at the screen, her voice echoing in the crowded Washington theatre. She became fixated on actress Joan Allen's portrayal of First Lady Pat Nixon, repeatedly yelling, "That is NOT Pat Nixon. I knew her, and she was NOT like that!" Of course, the rest of The Ladies had to add their two cents. Dorothy O rose from her seat, clapped her hands, and screamed, "Bravo, Helen! You tell them."

As we were exiting the movie theatre, a fellow movie viewer looked at Helen and said, "I thought I heard you commentating during the film, Helen!" Dorothy O added another "Bravo!"

Helen and The Ladies also liked to talk during stage plays. I vividly remember one occasion when Helen, Dorothy Newman, and I were in New York together. I was given tickets to see the play *Sherlock's Last Case*, which was on Broadway, by a family friend, theatre impresario Joe Nederlander. A friend and her parents who lived in a New York were invited to join us.

We got to the theatre early (Helen always had to arrive early when we saw plays), and everyone admired our "house" seats. Soon the play began, and almost immediately Helen was confused and could not follow what was taking place on the stage. She was especially perplexed by Sherlock Holmes' use of cocaine and kept asking me, "What is he doing?" I initially tried ignoring the questions for fear of disturbing others in the audience, but Helen's voice grew louder and more insistent. I finally whispered, "Cocaine." Helen would not let it drop, asking a series of related questions and wanting to converse as though we were in a restaurant or at home.

Finally, the people in the row in front of us became more than a little irritated. A woman turned around and motioning with her index finger in front of her nose, said, "Shhh!" Helen exclaimed, "Did you hear her? Who does she think she is? I will not be shushed!" Helen leaned forward into the back of the woman's neck and dramatically made her own shushing noises—repeatedly. The woman turned around again, and in a stage-whisper said, "Shut the hell up!" Helen moved forward in her seat, and I was becoming worried there would be trouble. My worries were averted when Dorothy leaned across my friends, and said, "For God's sake, Helen. Pipe down!"

Somehow, this quieted the situation, thankfully. After the play, we all went out to dinner, and nobody uttered a word about the incident.

The Cabin

Helen's husband, Doug Cornell, built a cabin in the Shenandoah Valley that was left to Helen after he died. Located deep in the woods outside Sperryville, Virginia, it was in a breathtaking setting. It bordered on Shenandoah National Park, so to access it, we had to drive up a fire trail that led to the park. There was a footbridge over a stream running in front of the cabin that had to be crossed from the cutout on the fire trail, and room for two cars where we parked. It was about an hour and a half from Washington, but it felt like a completely different world.

The cabin was comfortable but rustic. Once you got over the footbridge, there was a tree off to the right that had been given to Doug by Lady Bird Johnson. To the left, there were boulders that served as makeshift steps leading up to the cabin. You entered the cabin by way of a screened-in porch that led to the front door of the cabin. The inside consisted of a large living room with a stone fireplace taking up an entire wall. The decor was reminiscent of the late '60s or early '70s when it was built, complete with an ashtray hanging by a rope from the ceiling. The entire front was glass with a charming view of all that nature offered in the woods and the stream. There was an open kitchen with a wood table. It had one bathroom, and two bedrooms with twin beds in each.

There was a makeshift system of piping that brought a water supply up to the cabin from the stream. Sometimes the water worked, and other times it didn't. Regardless, the water was not potable.

Helen was never "outdoorsy," but she loved the cabin because it was built by her husband. My first summer staying with Helen, she suggested that her nieces (who lived in Washington) and I go to the cabin with her for the weekend. We packed up our bags, and all the food and supplies we needed, and hit the road. Helen's nieces were in the front, and Helen and I sat in the backseat of the car. As we neared the cabin, Helen suddenly picked up a magazine that was sitting on the seat between us. She held it close to her face for what seemed like an eternity. I finally asked what she was doing. There was no response, so I leaned over, and gently pulled the magazine down. Helen was in tears. When I asked what was wrong, she cried harder. Her nieces asked why she was crying. Helen finally told us, "Everything about this reminds me of Doug." It was Helen's first trip to the cabin after Doug died.

There were happier trips to the cabin over the years. Many of these involved The Ladies. They packed enough bags for a month, even though it was just a weekend trip, along with coolers filled with food, water, alcohol, and soft drinks. As the youngest member of the adventure, I hauled all of the items across the footbridge, up the boulder steps, through the porch, and into the living room. The Ladies took it from there.

One time, after many, many trips unloading things from the car, I entered the living room, and saw Dorothy O arguing with her sister about how to move one of the coolers filled with food from the living room into the kitchen. Dorothy said, "F*** you!" Gloria replied, "No, F*** YOU!" This continued for about three minutes until Helen chimed in, "Girls, let Diane move the cooler." Lucky me.

Typically, on the first night of these jaunts, The Ladies cooked dinner and invited the closest neighbors (who lived quite a hike away through the woods). They were an older couple who kept an eye on the cabin when nobody was there. They were extremely knowledgeable about all kinds of things found in the woods, including snakes and bears.

One night, I was telling the neighbors about how I had been frightened by a snake when I was sitting on the footbridge reading. My adrenaline "flight" response took over, and I bolted into the cabin. Helen was looking out the window, and despite my trying to enter the cabin calmly, she said, "Did you see a snake? Why were you running?" After relating all of this, the neighbor asked me if it was a poisonous snake. I said I didn't know. He asked if I could describe the snake. I said it looked like a snake. This went on for a while until Helen said, "A snake's a snake, and they have no business near this cabin." Everyone laughed, but I noticed The Ladies walked more cautiously the next day.

On another trip to the cabin with some friends my age, I was outside grilling when I heard CRUNCH, CRUNCH, CRUNCH in the woods. I ran into the cabin and told everyone there was a bear outside. My peers laughed at me, so I went outside and finished grilling. The following day we were invited to breakfast at the neighbors' house. When we got close, I noticed a wood pile strewn all over the place.

Opening the door, the neighbors greeted us with, "Did y'all see the big black bear last night? He messed up our wood pile."

I asked, "How big WAS the bear?"

She answered, "Just about the size of a large refrigerator." I gave a knowing look to my friends that said I wasn't crazy, after all.

The second evening at the cabin, The Ladies would get all gussied up to dine at The Inn at Little Washington, a highly rated restaurant about a 20-minute drive from our rustic setting. The irony of putting on nice clothes in a cabin where we couldn't even drink the water often hit me.

Located in the foothills of the Blue Ridge Mountains, The Inn at Little Washington is a gastronomic experience, and the beauty of The Inn only adds to the experience. Built in the late 19th century as a gas station, The Inn was transformed into a restaurant in the late '70s, and The Ladies discovered it immediately. All of The Ladies enjoyed good food, particularly good food with a nice ambiance.

The Ladies would eat course after course at The Inn at Little Washington. Helen was especially fond of sweet breads and would always try to share this delicacy with me. Over my protests, she would put some on my plate, and I would choke it back. I finally had to tell her I don't do sweet breads—or any organ meat!

Dorothy O was always in seventh heaven at The Inn. She fancied herself a chef and would ask our waiter to see the real chef, Patrick O'Connell. He dutifully came to our table and answered a long list of Dorothy's questions while everyone else at the table shifted uncomfortably in their seats.

I always had to laugh at one of the highlights of dining at this exquisite French restaurant. Because we couldn't drink the water at the cabin, many of us brought our toothbrushes with us, and brushed our teeth in the ladies' room at The Inn. Everyone enjoyed the food, and clean teeth!

Upon returning to the cabin, The Ladies would have a roaring fire in the stone fireplace if the weather was cool enough. They laughed, and talked, and simply enjoyed each other's company.

Several storms caused damage to the cabin, the footbridge, and the surrounding property over the years. It was difficult for Helen to get the repairs made with her busy life and being so far away. The second time the footbridge was washed away, she decided to sell the cabin. It was a hard decision since it was all she had left from her years with Doug. However, she decided to move ahead, and she sold it to a lovely couple. Years later, I took a trip to Sperryville with some friends, and we visited the cabin. We were taking in the view from the other side of the bridge when the new owners approached us. They allowed us to look inside the cabin. I was grateful it looked pretty much as I remembered it—though the hanging ashtray was no longer there.

Mama Ayesha's

Helen's home away from home was a restaurant originally known as Calvert Cafe—it is now called Mama Ayesha's—and Helen always referred to it simply as "Ayesha's." Anyone who knew Helen inevitably spent a lot of time there.

Born in the late 1800s, Ayesha Abraham was a Palestinian woman from the Mount of Olives. Her house overlooked the Old City of Jerusalem. Legend has it (according to Helen), Ayesha was caught by the King of Jordan raising pigs to sell to the servicemen (her land was under the control of Jordan at that time). This did not go over well in a Muslim country, both because pork was forbidden and because she was a woman. Because the King was after her, Ayesha was forced to escape in the darkness of night, leaving everything behind. She ended up in Washington after traveling through England and Canada.

Ayesha arrived in the Nation's Capital in the 1940s and found a job at the Syrian embassy as a cook. Helen was invited to a party at the embassy and complimented the ambassador on the food being served, telling him it reminded her of her mother's cooking. The ambassador responded by explaining their new cook had quite an ego, and he asked Helen if he could introduce the two of them so Helen could compliment Ayesha directly. Ayesha appeared, and Helen told her the food was delicious. Ayesha said, "I know. I made it." A friendship was born.

By 1960, after working at the embassy and several restaurants, Ayesha was ready to open her own restaurant. However, there was one obstacle. She needed a loan, so Helen arranged for Ayesha to meet her friend Dorothy Newman, a real estate broker with bank connections. Dorothy convinced a Jewish bank president, Leo Bernstein, to meet with the Palestinian woman in need of money to start her restaurant.

On the scheduled day of the meeting, Dorothy picked up Ayesha, who, as usual, was wearing her native clothes and braided pig tails. The meeting went well enough until Mr. Bernstein asked Ayesha what she had as collateral for the loan. Ayesha thought about it and offered a ring she was wearing on her finger. She got the loan, and the Calvert Cafe opened soon thereafter.

The restaurant went through many machinations. In the early days, Ayesha not only ran the place, but as Helen used to say, "She was the chief cook and bottle washer." During the Vietnam era, a lot of men crowded the restaurant before they left for the war, and Ayesha would declare, "Drinks are on the house!" Henry Kissinger ate at the restaurant, and because English was a second language for Ayesha, she called him "Dr. Kussinger." During the Carter era, high-level White

House officials frequented the place, including Carter's press secretary and trusted advisor, Jody Powell.

Ayesha was quite proud when she became an American citizen, and she celebrated her "Pomegration Day" (Ayesha's term for the day she became a citizen) every Valentine's Day with a heart-shaped cake. She shared the cake with family and friends, and even some customers.

By the time I came to Washington, Ayesha's was in full swing, and Helen ate there two or three nights a week, sometimes more. Helen had a table in a corner of the restaurant that was always reserved for her, and nobody dared sit there unless they were dining with her. It was a long, banquet-sized table that could accommodate as few or as many guests as Helen hosted.

Meals were usually eaten in courses, and they always included appetizers selected by Helen for the table to share with drinks. These usually were composed of some combination of hummus, grape leaves, and a tomato and onion salad—which everyone referred to as Helen's salad, and it is listed as such on the menu today.

Everyone was on their own to order an entree. After the others had ordered, Helen would ask the waiter, "What's fresh?" The waiter recited the food prepared for Ayesha and her many relatives who worked at the restaurant. But Helen's all-time favorite meal had nothing to do with the menu: steak and hand-cut French fries—which she typically asked me to share.

Dessert consisted of a plate of sweets such as baklava or bird's nest for sharing, followed by fresh fruit. This course was always served with traditional Arab coffee—so Ayesha could read the coffee grounds. The ritual involved turning the cup three times while placing the cup upside down on the saucer, making a wish, and letting the cup dry with some of the sludge left in the bottom.

Ayesha sat in a chair close to Helen's table, holding court. Helen had her cup read every night she was at Ayesha's. Ayesha never told her anything bad, and Helen always had "a bright future," according to Ayesha's readings. A couple of times, Ayesha was right on the money. One evening, Helen had her cup read. She was supposed to leave the following morning on a presidential trip on Air Force One. Ayesha said in her fractured English, "You not going. President's trip cancelled." Helen thought Ayesha was just wishing Helen wouldn't go away, so she would come to the restaurant. Helen said, "Oh, yes. I will be on the trip, but I'll come see you as soon as I get back." Ayesha insisted there would be no trip. Later, Helen got word the president had cancelled the trip.

I don't care for the taste of coffee, so I never tried the much stronger Arabic coffee until one evening in 1984. I worked on the Mondale-Ferraro election campaign. The day before the election, some of my colleagues and I went to Ayesha's for dinner, even though we had to leave for Minnesota early the next morning (where Fritz Mondale was from). At the end of dinner, my campaign friends cajoled me into doing a cup of coffee so Ayesha could read my cup. I acquiesced, choking back the coffee in one gulp.

I had never heard Ayesha "read" anything negative in

anybody's cup, but there is a first for everything. When I took my cup to Ayesha, she was initially surprised since I had never had my cup read before. She said, "Dee-on, you have your cup read?" Ayesha always pronounced my name with her accent. I told her my friends wanted me to have my cup read. After looking into the cup, turning it around several times, looking in it again, Ayesha proclaimed, "Your candidate not going to win!" She was right, but this did not sit well with my campaign coworkers!

I was still living with Helen while I worked on that presidential campaign, but I was rarely home. However, when I was at Helen's, it sometimes created awkward situations. I remember one such instance when a reporter covering the campaign reached me late one night on Helen's home phone (this was well before cell phones). Helen answered, and knew the reporter calling me. She came into my room and stayed while I was on the phone, listening intently to the information I gave the journalist. After I hung up, Helen said, "I'd like to clarify some things you were saying." Always a reporter, Helen got the scoop that the other reporter thought was an exclusive.

Over the years, I met a lot of interesting people with Helen at Ayesha's. There were dinners with prominent politicians such as presidents and first ladies, members of Congress and senators. There were cabinet members and an assortment of high-profile journalists. There were even Hollywood celebrities.

One of the most memorable dinners was with a group of women from Hollywood. Bea Arthur, Betty White,

Brenda Vaccaro, Lily Tomlin, and Lily's long-time partner (now wife) and comedy collaborator, Jane Wagner, were in town to attend a PETA protest, and one of them called Helen to see if she could have dinner with them.

I received a call earlier in the day from Helen telling me I "had" to meet her at Ayesha's to have dinner with a group of women who were in town. When I saw who the women were, I was a little shocked Helen had not mentioned who was coming, but this was typical of her. It seems I only knew who some of the women were, however. This was no surprise to those who knew me. I've always been more familiar with politicians than celebrities. As conversation began, one of the women asked what I did for a living. After explaining that I was a literary agent, I turned to her to reciprocate the question. And asked, "So, what do you do?" The woman replied, "I am an actress." I later learned that Brenda Vaccaro was, indeed, an actress—and well known. Admittedly, sometimes I live under a pop-culture rock the size of a boulder.

Helen was seated next to Bea Arthur, and I periodically observed Helen sort of "jumping" in her seat. I tried to figure out what was happening, and I looked in Helen's eyes quizzically. Afterward, Helen told me that the actress was rubbing Helen's thigh, and Helen was convinced Bea was "hitting" on her.

As the evening wore on, Bea Arthur went to the restroom. When she came out, she had a long piece of toilet paper flowing from the back of her pants. I looked at Helen, and she shook her head back and forth as if to say, "Don't say anything." I didn't utter a word, nor did anyone else at the table! Bea left the restaurant with the toilet paper still hanging from her backside. Helen later said she didn't want any further interaction with Bea, not even to help her with the indelicate situation.

Despite all the fun, there was a downside to eating with Helen at Ayesha's. Word had gotten out that this was Helen's hangout. Customers came to the restaurant just to meet her, and some of them were fairly rude. Many of them would take a seat at Helen's table in the extra chairs not being used—and expect to have dinner with us. Helen had a habit of befriending perfect strangers and inviting them to dinner, but these were NOT invited people. Even for Helen, some of the people's behavior was over the top, and she would rely on me to get them to leave the table. I got better at this over time. Helen would give me "the look"—and I would say, "We have both enjoyed meeting you, but if you will excuse us, we have some business to discuss." Sometimes my comment worked, and other times, the strangers would simply ignore me.

Several incidents that occurred at Ayesha's could not be ignored. Helen and I happened to be eating in the restaurant after the domestic terrorism bombing in Oklahoma City. Helen noticed an olive-skinned man sitting alone in a booth. He was crying. Helen got up from our table to see if the man was all right. In tears, he explained how he was stopped by police and taken into custody. After hours of questioning by police about whether he had been in Oklahoma City, he was let go. He was upset that his "only crime" was that he was of

Arab background. This moved Helen, and she invited him to join us.

This wasn't the only time I saw blatant discrimination based on olive skin tone. Helen and I were dining at Ayesha's when we heard commotion coming from a door off the kitchen. Someone standing near the door began screaming for help. Helen asked me to go find out what was happening. When I got to the door, I witnessed a metro cop beating up Ayesha's nephew, who managed the restaurant. The cop was repeating over and over again, "Do you see the color of my skin? It is white. Your skin is not white." I flew back inside and dialed 911. I told the operator to send police because a metro policeman was beating someone up. She said, "You mean someone is beating up the metro policeman?" I said, "No! I mean the cop is beating up the manager of the restaurant!" Two other policemen eventually arrived and pulled the metro cop off of Ayesha's nephew, whose shirt was ripped in several places. The "bad" cop was allowed to get back in his cruiser and leave. Helen and I spoke with the responding officers, and I told them what I had witnessed. Their solution was to reassign the "bad" cop to airport duty. I didn't think he should have gotten off so easily, but at least the crisis was over.

There was another time I called 911 from the restaurant. I was having dinner with a friend when Ayesha's sister, Sophie, who worked in the back, came out from the kitchen and collapsed. A large crowd gathered around her. A few minutes passed, and Ayesha yelled over to me. When I saw Sophie was still lying on the floor, I called 911. The paramedics suspected a heart attack and were going to take her by ambulance to the hospital. Ayesha said to me, "You go with her."

Realizing there was no time to waste, I grabbed my purse and asked my friend if she could come with me. We rode in the ambulance with Sophie, and when we arrived at George Washington University Hospital, Sophie was whisked to the back. After waiting a long time, someone came out and asked, "Who is with the woman who only speaks Arabic?" I knew that was my cue, but I did not speak Arabic. I was escorted to the curtained off area where I saw Sophie. She smiled when she saw me. I have no idea how I communicated with her, but I managed to comfort her enough to calm her down.

The doctors determined that Sophie needed a pacemaker, so I called the restaurant and spoke with Ayesha's nephew. We were at the hospital all night, and the following day, when I knew Sophie was going to be okay, I called Helen to let her know what had taken place. Helen came to the hospital immediately, and she told me to go home and get some much-needed sleep.

Ayesha was grateful I spent the time with her sister. I'm not sure if the next turn of events was her way of showing gratitude or not. I had a new kitten, and I was telling Helen about her one evening at the restaurant. Helen was afraid of cats and dogs, but she always acted interested in what I was up to. Unbeknownst to either of us, Ayesha had overheard our conversation. She called me over, and said, "Bring the cat to me so I can see." Confused, I answered, "You want me to bring my kitten to the restaurant?" Ayesha replied, "Yes. Tomorrow." Helen told me she thought Ayesha was serious, so the following evening, we returned to Ayesha's with my kitten in a carrying case. Ayesha cooed at the kitten, holding her. The kitten purred. I asked Helen if she wanted to hold the kitten, too. Helen said, "I think I'll just admire her from here!"

There were other "moments" at the restaurant caused by Ayesha herself. Once, during one of the many conflicts in the Middle East, Ayesha answered the phone at the restaurant. When she hung up, she called for her nephew and said, "Take me home!" Ayesha never left until closing time, so this was concerning. Everyone asked if she felt ill. Ayesha said she felt fine but continued to demand she be taken home. When her nephew returned after dropping off Ayesha at her house, the phone rang again. It was Ayesha. She said, "Did the bomb go off yet?" Helen concluded, "Now. That's self-preservation!" Ayesha always had quite an ego.

The only other time Ayesha asked to be taken home early was two days before she passed away in 1993. Helen missed her "second mother" terribly, but we continued to frequent the restaurant. Ayesha left the restaurant to her nephews, who were already working in the family business. The year after Ayesha passed away, the restaurant was renamed "Mama Ayesha's" in honor of its founder. It is still in its original location and continues to serve Ayesha's recipes. "Helen's Salad" is still on the menu, too.

Entertaining, Black-Tie and White-Tie Dinners

Helen loved to entertain, and she was a good cook. In fact, often her bedtime reading consisted of cookbooks. Her meals were old fashioned, featuring heavy, fattening foods, and they were delicious. Helen was particularly adept at making potatoes. I used to love her stovetop, fried potatoes, and her Yukon Gold mashed potatoes dripping in butter and heavy cream. She frequently enjoyed hosting small, intimate dinner parties at her home. Because she did the cooking, I was on cleanup duty, clearing the table, and doing the dishes, including the voluminous number of pots and pans left with hardened grit and food. But I didn't mind since these get-togethers were interesting.

Helen had people over for lunch only occasionally, and only on weekends due to her busy schedule covering the White House. She typically served soup and her version of tea sandwiches: white bread with the crust removed, ham, and mayonnaise. I could never believe the mess she could make in the kitchen with these sandwiches.

Helen especially liked to host parties for holidays. We spent Thanksgiving with The Ladies, Helen's nieces (and their families) who lived in the area, and assorted friends. Helen did most of the cooking in the early days, but she had Ayesha's nephew deliver a turkey he cooked (he was a trained chef). As Helen got older, Thanksgiving moved to my place, but Helen still arranged for the turkey to be delivered.

One Thanksgiving, I stayed over at a friend's house the night before. This had become somewhat of a tradition for a group of friends when we were in our early 20s. We always went out to dinner the night before Thanksgiving, and then we would talk into the wee hours of the morning at their college-like group house. When the phone rang in the morning, I was surprised to hear it was Helen's niece asking for me. When I picked up the phone, her niece told me that "Aunt Helen" had cut her finger chopping some food for Thanksgiving later that day. She thought Helen needed stitches, but Helen refused to go to the hospital. I asked if I should talk to Helen on the phone, and her niece said she thought it would be better if I got to Helen's place as soon as possible.

I jumped in my car and drove the half-hour to get to Helen's. When I arrived, Helen was sitting on her bed with her finger wrapped in paper towels. Blood had seeped through. Helen asked if I would look at her finger. I felt I had no choice, so hesitantly, I unwound the wad of paper towels. As soon as I saw her finger, I said, "Let's get this checked out." Leaving no room for negotiation, and over Helen's objections, I stood there with Helen's purse in hand. We went to the emergency room, and Helen ended up with quite a few stitches. That evening when friends and family were gathered for the turkey feast, Helen told everyone I had saved her life. She was not usually prone to this type of exaggeration, but I guess the "trauma" of the ER visit had warped her sense of reality.

Years later, I thought of the finger episode when Helen broke a metatarsal bone in her foot. Apparently, she was walking to the corner drugstore when she slipped on a wet leaf. She hobbled home, and I received a panicked call asking me to come over as quickly as possible. I still had a key to her condo, so I let myself in. Helen was perched on the sofa, crying. Her foot was swollen so I got her some ice and told her to elevate her foot. Then I tried to persuade her to get an X-ray. She refused to go to the hospital, so I called a friend who was a podiatrist. She agreed to come into her office on a Sunday to X-ray Helen's foot. She put Helen in a Velcro boot. One thing Helen and I had in common was being frightened of doctors.

On another Thanksgiving, Helen asked me to bring homemade pumpkin pies. This posed a problem since my kitchen and I are not all that well acquainted, and I had never baked a pie in my entire life. A friend had an idea. We bought some frozen pies at the grocery store, baked them off, and I told Helen my friend's mother had made them. I got away with my fib until the next time Helen saw my friend's mom. Helen went on and on about how delicious the pies tasted. Luckily for me, my friend's mom suspected something was up, and she went along with it. A couple of days later when my friend and I were alone with her mother, her mom remarked, "I hope I'm never asked to bake a pie for Helen since she might notice the difference. What were you girls thinking?"

Helen also gave an annual Christmas party, originally at Ayesha's, for friends, family, colleagues, and other assorted people she met in her travels. Guests' children were included in the festivities, and one of my friends played Santa Claus for the children—and for some adults who liked to have photos taken sitting on Santa's lap. Eventually, the number of people invited outgrew what Ayesha's could handle, so it was moved to a private room at the National Press Club.

Regardless of the venue, I sometimes felt like a party planner with little or no guidance. My mom designed, printed, and addressed the invitations to the party—after I hunted down addresses for the names of people I didn't know on Helen's scribbled guest list. Helen added to the guest list almost every day for a month, but even at that, there were still others invited after the invitations were sent. After the first couple of years, my mom and I knew to give Helen dozens of extra invitations since she seemed to be standing on the street corner asking strangers if they wanted to attend her party. Unfortunately, that is not much of an exaggeration.

The next step in my party planner role was figuring out party favors, and again, I eventually came to realize

I needed dozens of extra items since Helen never knew who she had invited, or how many. I bought holiday-themed coloring books and crayons for the younger children and came up with assorted ideas for the adults. One year, when the party favor was a hand-blown Christmas ornament, a friend's little boy observed some people stealing other guests' favors. They were not people I knew, and we never saw them again. I am sure they were people Helen only met once or twice.

Relatively speaking, working with Ayesha's or the National Press Club to pick a menu based on Helen's likes and dislikes was easy. Helen was not fond of most vegetables, so I would arbitrarily pick one I thought went with the meat and potatoes Helen preferred. She had more input when the party was at Ayesha's since we were there so often.

The most dreadful part of the Christmas party was figuring out the place cards, which Helen insisted were necessary. The trouble was not so much in putting people together who knew one another, but in the fact that Helen sometimes did not know the names of people she invited. One year, she invited some people from the Mexican embassy, and she did not know any of their names. When I asked what I should put on the place cards, she told me, "Just put the word 'Mexican' on them." So that's what I did.

Helen loved to sing, so during the years the party was at the Press Club, I arranged for a piano and pianist to play Christmas carols. The guests all gathered around the piano, with Helen leading the singing. Everyone loved it.

Some people brought gifts to the party for Helen, and I was the recipient of presents from The Ladies. Some of these gifts were quite unusual, particularly those from Dorothy O. Two packages that stand out were a can of soup and a thumb-sized container of carpet cleaner. I wrote her a thank-you note both times proclaiming how delicious the soup tasted and how "fresh" my carpet smelled.

One holiday Helen didn't entertain for was Easter. Instead, she provided the "access" to the annual White House Easter Egg Roll for me to take her great-niece and great-nephew. Helen "cleared in" to the White House my trio, as well as a friend or two and their young children so we didn't have to wait in the line to get in that sometimes went for blocks.

The original Easter Monday tradition dates back a long time. The first White House Easter Egg Roll took place under President Rutherford B. Hayes, but the modern-day custom of children in attendance hunting for souvenir, wooden eggs was begun under President Ronald Reagan. The event takes place on the South Lawn of the White House. It is a children's event, but the adults embrace it, too. Activities vary from year to year, and most years feature characters walking on stilts. One year as I held one of Helen's great-nephews on my shoulders, we came across the character of Uncle Sam and the child on my shoulders asked me, "Who is Uncle Sam?" I was stumped as to how to answer, so I said he was a symbol of our American government. This led to a number of "whys," until, thankfully, I was eventually saved when the child spotted a wooden egg.

In addition to giving parties, Helen was generous in inviting friends and family to attend the "season" of Washington's annual dinners. First up every year was The Congressional Dinner, put on by the Washington Press Club Foundation. It is an evening meant to bring together members of the media with Capitol Hill.

Guests included Helen's nieces and their husbands, and senators, members of Congress, and White House officials. Helen always asked me to go in the ballroom with her where the dinner was being held to put the place cards on the table during the cocktail reception. From what I observed, Helen's table was the only one with place cards. And, again, sometimes Helen invited people whom she did not know, or even intended to invite.

One year, Helen wanted to invite a certain senator, a Democrat, but instead, she inadvertently invited a different senator, a Republican, with a similar sounding name. She realized her error when the Republican senator called Helen to ask if he could bring his wife. To top things off, Helen put my place card next to the Republican senator as she said, "You handle him!" He and his wife ended up being pleasant enough.

Among the memorable moments at the Congressional Dinner was the time Helen's table was next to a table hosted by *People* magazine that included Supreme Court Justice Sandra Day O'Connor. All of a sudden, there was a ruckus at the table, and we overheard John Riggins, a running back for the Washington Redskins, tell the first female justice, "Loosen up, Sandy baby," as he fell to the floor. He slept on the floor throughout all the speeches taking place at the podium, including that of then Vice President George H.W. Bush. Justice O'Connor seemed to take it all in stride, but Helen was aghast.

Another memorable time was when Sonny Bono was a freshman member of Congress, and he spoke at the dinner. The rambling beginning of his speech, sometimes with slurred words, made the high-powered audience uncomfortable. Rep. Bono explained how he got involved in politics. He was opening a restaurant, and he needed a sign, so he went to the city office in Palm Springs to get a permit for the sign. He was instructed to fill out a form and come back the following day. When he went back to the city office the next day, he was told to come back in a week. Then he was told to come back in three weeks. Bono explained that he was beginning to dislike the city government official. In desperation, he told the official, "I'm going to run for mayor, and fire you!" This brought down the house with laughter erupting in the room. Bono told the audience he did run for mayor and fired the city employee. He added that he wasn't entirely heartless because "he's my gardener now."

Helen's favorite dinner was the Gridiron's annual white-tie dinner. The Gridiron Club's exclusive membership is made up of 65 active members from print and broadcasting organizations, though the membership was originally limited to print journalists. One has to be invited to join the club, and Helen used to say a member had to die before another journalist could be asked to join. Helen was its first female member and first female president.

The Gridiron Club is best known for its annual white-tie dinner held in the spring. All of the "who's who" of Washington usually attend the dinner, from the sitting president to Supreme Court justices to senators and members of Congress.

In addition to many courses of food and wine at the dinner, members of the club perform two satirical musical skits—one Republican, the other Democratic. They change the words to familiar songs and poke fun at politicians and current events. Helen absolutely loved performing in these skits. When she was assigned her role, she practiced her songs—continuously—and everywhere. She burst into song at Ayesha's and other restaurants. She practiced singing at my place, at her place, and at friends' homes. It paid off. Helen's performances usually brought down the house at the yearly dinners.

My mom and dad were invited (with me) to attend for so many years that the performances began to blur together, but we still appreciated being invited. However, nobody was particularly keen on the "elegant" food served. One year, after looking over the menu at each place setting, the man seated next to me turned and said, "So, tonight we will be eating Thumper and Bambi. Can't we have something edible?"

Helen's guests at the Gridiron usually included her friend ABC newsman Sam Donaldson, as well as advice columnist Dear Abby. On one occasion, Dear Abby and I went to the restroom together between the two musical skits. Abby was not getting along with her twin sister, Ann Landers, who also wrote a syndicated advice column. As usual, there was a long line to get into the bathroom. Abby and I were chatting when she suddenly jumped out of the line, motioning with her head to a few people ahead of us. There was Ann Landers. Abby whispered that she didn't want to create a scene. I assured her there would not be a scene, and there was not. However, the following day in *The Washington Post's* coverage of the dinner, there was a photo of Ann Landers—identified as Dear Abby. This did not please Abby, and she claimed she was going to ask *The Post* for a correction. I am not sure if Abby ever made the request, but I never saw a correction printed. Years later, Dear Abby reconciled with her sister.

In 1993, when Helen became the first female president of the Gridiron Club, she was to open the evening with the "Speech in the Dark," a tradition where the lights are turned off while the new president of the club addresses the guests in attendance. Bill Clinton was the president of the United States, and he was scheduled to speak and play the saxophone at the dinner. A holding area had been set up where Helen was supposed to greet President Clinton, but he was late, or as Helen put it, "He was running on Clinton time."

Rather than further delay the start to the already long night, Helen decided to get the evening going. But just as she stepped up to the podium, and the lights were dimmed, someone grabbed her to tell her President Clinton had arrived. She stepped off the podium and went to the holding area. President Clinton said,

"Before we go in, I'd like to wet my whistle." Helen thought to herself, "After arriving late, he wants a drink?" It took a moment to figure out the president wanted to practice his saxophone!

The next dinner in the season was the White House Correspondents' Association's Dinner, traditionally held on the last Saturday in April. This black-tie occasion is always held at the Washington Hilton on Connecticut Avenue and is Washington's answer to the Oscars. Put on by the journalists who cover the White House, it is the highest-profile dinner of all the annual dinners. Helen was the White House Correspondents' Association's first female member and its first female president. She was instrumental in getting women to be allowed to attend the dinner when she convinced President Kennedy to decline to attend the dinner unless women were included. The president and vice president are usually in attendance.

The evening features a comedic speech by the sitting president, followed by a high-profile entertainer. It is such a hot ticket and the ballroom is so overcrowded that in order for people to squeeze between tables, it is often necessary for guests to get up from their chairs to let someone pass. I always thought the fire marshal might shut the dinner down.

As the Dean of the White House press corps, Helen was usually at the head table in front of the room with the current president of the Association, and the president of the United States. Helen invited guests to the dinner who sat in the audience, and she always allowed me to invite friends to come as well.

The evening begins with a red-carpet arrival with working media behind velvet rope lines. Helen would dutifully walk the red carpet, blowing kisses to her fans, and stopping for an occasional interview. In her older years when she didn't walk as well, she would hold my arm or hand for balance. I would try to stay out of the TV camera shots, but many friends told me they spotted me.

It was an extremely exciting evening, beginning with pre-parties and ending with post-parties sponsored by news organizations. As Helen got older, she did not care for the mob scene at the post-parties, so we would spread the word to friends that she would be in one of the bars in the hotel after the dinner. Thirty to forty people would gather in the bar as Helen held court, discussing the highlights of the dinner, and the political topics of the day. We usually closed the bar.

I had some memorable things happen during the dinner. One year, I was on crutches due to a broken ankle. My college roommate was in town for the dinner, and she convinced the Secret Service agents working the dinner to allow me to crutch through the holding area for the president when I had to use the restroom. Our table was not close to the door to exit the ballroom, so it would have been difficult to get through the crowd.

My college roommate and I started through the holding area with Secret Service agents surrounding us. We were about halfway through the cordoned off area when I suddenly felt my skirt begin to slip off (I was wearing a two-piece, black ensemble). I abruptly stopped crutching to hold up the skirt. The agents kept repeating, "You have to keep moving," but in order to keep moving on crutches, I needed my hands—one of which was being used to keep my skirt from falling off. My friend repeated the request, asking, "Did you hear them?" I whispered to her about my predicament, and she grabbed my skirt, and said, "Okay. Crutch on." Somehow, I made it to the bathroom, and I felt like the luckiest person alive when someone offered me safety pins in the restroom. Helen roared with laughter when we relayed the story to her at the bar afterward.

On another occasion, I was again on crutches (the same injury lasted a while). This time, I decided to maneuver through the packed room on my own to use the bathroom. There is a slightly elevated area that runs along the perimeter of the ballroom, and it is also crowded with tables of people attending the dinner. I crutched up the few steps to get a view of how I might be able to cut a path to the exit. As I scanned the room, someone accidentally bumped into me. I lost my balance, my crutches went flying, and I tumbled down the stairs. As I pathetically tried to collect myself, a woman spoke to me from behind, and asked, "Are you all right? My husband is a doctor, and I can get him to help you." Embarrassed, I turned to address the kind woman to tell her I was okay. Much to my surprise, the nice woman was Mary Tyler Moore! In subsequent years, when I ran into her, she always asked, "How's that ankle doing?"

I was on and off crutches for years, and there was one other time when I was on them for the White House Correspondents' Dinner. This time, a friend who was an off-duty Secret Service agent was one of our guests. When I inevitably had to use the ladies' room, the agent offered to go with me to clear a path. She was more than proficient at doing so, walking in front of me and asking people to let me through. As we were passing a table where Bill Richardson, former governor of New Mexico and then commerce secretary, was sitting, he recognized my friend as a Secret Service agent, and asked in a perplexed way, "Who *is* that woman, and why does she have Secret Service protection?" I felt like the VIP of all VIPs!

Another highlight of the year was attending the White House Christmas party. Every year, they throw a series of parties during the holidays hosted by the president and first lady. There are several parties for the media, and I was fortunate to attend many of these with Helen throughout her tenure covering the White House.

There is nothing like the White House decked out with festive decorations at Christmas. Ever since First Lady Jackie Kennedy, all first ladies have picked a theme that ties the decor together. After the September 11 tragedy, the White House had a red, white, and blue theme chosen by First Lady Laura Bush based on letters the White House received.

Even in years when the decor was not the best, it was always wonderful to be there. Decorated trees with lights illuminating the state rooms and a huge gingerbread replica of the White House were always some of the highlights. Cocktail tables were available in the East Room and State Dining Room to enjoy the delicious food, which always included the largest shrimp known to mankind. The experience was like being dropped into a winter wonderland.

The main feature of the decorations was always the Christmas tree in the Blue Room. It is so tall that the crystal chandelier has to be removed in the room to allow it to fit. President William Taft's children are believed to have begun the tradition of placing the tree in the Blue Room, and there is a national competition judged by the National Christmas Tree Association to decide which state's tree has the honor of adorning the Blue Room.

There is always a receiving line to greet the sitting president and first lady and have a photo taken with them. Because the line could be long, the Clinton administration began giving out a card with a specific time to go through the receiving line. A military aide announces each guest's name before they approach the presidential couple.

One year, President Clinton injured his knee, and while we were waiting in the receiving line, Helen inquired, "What are you going to ask the president?" I told her I was going to ask how his knee was doing. Just as the military aide was about to announce our names, Helen turned to me and said, "I think I'll take your idea," leaving me scrambling to come up with another topic.

My all-time favorite White House Christmas party was one I did not attend, but it exemplified Helen's big heart for people less privileged. I brought my parents' handyman, Dick, to Washington to do a number of projects around my home. He was extremely talented, and he could do anything from electrical work to plumbing to laying floors to building furniture—and everything between. Because Dick was staying with me while he was working on my place, he often joined me for dinner with Helen, usually at Ayesha's.

After observing how good Dick's work was, Helen asked if Dick could stay a couple of weeks longer to get some things done around her place. He consented, and our dinners together continued. During one of our dinners, Helen invited me to the White House Christmas party. Dick's eyes grew wider, and he commented, "That must be really something to see the White House this time of year." Helen and I told him about what it was like, and Dick's interest took off. White House Christmas parties was the only topic of conversation throughout dinner.

The following day, Helen called me, and said, "How about if I take Dick to the party instead of you? It would be my way of repaying him for extending his stay for me." I readily agreed. That evening, the three of us met for dinner again so Helen could invite Dick to the White House. He was so overwhelmed with joy that Helen and I noticed him tearing up. However, Dick had one concern. He only had his "work clothes" with him, and those consisted of blue jeans, paint-speckled sweatshirts, and baseball caps.

We arranged for one of Dick's neighbors who had a key to his house to overnight Dick's "best" clothes. The package arrived with a plaid, flannel shirt, ripped sport coat, khaki pants, "passable" brown shoes, and no tie. I thought to myself, "This is never going to work, and I do not want Helen to be embarrassed."

When I called Helen to tell her about Dick's wardrobe, she said, "Take him shopping!" I bought him a nice suit, white shirt, and tie. He was all set for the party—until his nerves set in. The day of the party, Dick was worried he "wouldn't fit in." Helen and I assured him there was nothing to worry about. I sent him out the door looking great, and he had the time of his life.

Helen arranged to get Dick's photo with the first couple from the White House and my mom had it framed for him. Dick carried the framed photo with him in his work van until he died, proudly showing it to all of his customers. Helen and I agreed it was well worth all the effort.

Speeches

Helen was a regular on the lecture circuit, at times giving as many as three speeches a week. She was good, and the audiences loved hearing her remarks about covering the White House, and about journalism, in general. She was funny, yet poignant, in what she said.

Helen never had adequate computer skills. In fact, some of her younger colleagues at the White House would privately complain to me when returning from presidential trips that Helen was constantly asking them for help filing her stories. So, when it came to writing speeches, Helen would ask me to set up the computer with "speech type," an oversized font so she could easily see her copy while talking.

One of the earliest times I heard Helen speak was at my high school graduation. I was a class officer, and because the other class officers knew about my internships and living with Helen, it was decided Helen would be a good choice to speak at our commencement. So, Helen was the class of 1980's graduation speaker at Kingswood School Cranbrook (now known as Cranbrook-Kingswood). Helen gave me her speech afterward, and it is the only speech Helen gave that I saved in full. Here are some excerpts:

I know you have come of age in the television era and the real world as it is today is not so remote. We have had a daily diet of village bombings during the Vietnam War; of rampant violence, terror, the Iranian hostage crisis, the brutal invasion of Afghanistan. You have seen a president resign his office in disgrace during the Watergate scandal, and a nation split asunder in the turbulent '60s with protest marches, and the civil rights movement. You have seen a nation survive. All that, and more. You have seen history....

One has but to look around to see the challenges that cry out for greater involvement and a greater commitment on the part of young people, especially the educated. You're breaking ground in the '80s. It is your decade. It can be an era that lights the way to a greater push to make this land we love even more true to the ideals of freedom and humanity for which this country was founded....

In the struggle for civil rights, equal rights for women, equal opportunity for blacks and Hispanics and the underprivileged, we know the job is far from done to make this a more perfect nation. But in all these struggles, there are profiles in courage. Even during the most brutal period of the civil rights march on Selma, reporters saw King go through a restaurant where his followers had gathered with a paper bag in his hand. He made them drop their guns and knives into the bag—to pursue the ideal of non-violence....

Women chained themselves to the White House fence in the suffragette era to win the vote.... I believe women have the talents and capacity to rise to all the great occasions, like even being president of the United States, and why not?

As I watch the passing parade at the White House, I am convinced that a woman in the Oval Office is not beyond the realm—someday.... The demands are great on those who aspire to public office. But it can be, as Kennedy said, "the crown of a career." In a president, we know the highest integrity is required—indeed indispensable.... I never walk through the White House gates without a sense of awe. I am lucky to have picked a career in which each day has been an education....

To everything there is a season. For the graduates, your day has come. And each day can be an adventure. Leave the prosaic and the pragmatic to others. Dream dreams of things that never were and ask, "Why not?" The future is in your hands....

My graduating classmates, parents, teachers, and others in the audience all congratulated Helen for a terrific, meaningful commencement address. And I could not have been happier to have Helen with me on such a significant day.

Helen opened her speeches after she was introduced by saying, "It's hard to hear your own obituary." She usually had an underlying message to her speeches, but she mixed it up with funny or meaningful stories about noted political people she encountered. She ran through these in the order of the administrations she covered. The following are some of the interesting anecdotes I recall:

On President John F. Kennedy:
"When I asked John F. Kennedy if he wanted his boy,

John John, to grow up to be president, he said, 'I just want him to be healthy.'"

"My favorite president was JFK. He was inspired. He said we could send a man to the moon. People thought he was crazy. He didn't live to see it, but we did it."

On First Lady Jacqueline Kennedy:
"When we sent a note to Jacqueline Kennedy asking her what she fed her new German Shepherd, she wrote back, 'Reporters.'"

On President Lyndon B. Johnson:
"When Johnson delivered an eloquent address at Gettysburg during the height of racial strife in this country, he said, 'We shall overcome.'"

"When LBJ had his gallbladder removed at Walter Reed, the psychiatric ward was converted to a press room. We asked him what they did with all the patients, and he said, 'We gave them all press passes.'"

"When a speechwriter was asked to prepare a certain speech for LBJ, he looked it over, and said, 'Voltaire? The people don't know Voltaire.' He picked up a pen, crossed it out, and wrote in its place, 'As my dear, old daddy used to say.'"

"I was invited to dinner in the family quarters of the White House with a small group that included LBJ's press secretary, Bill Moyers, an ordained minister. President Johnson asked Moyers to say grace. As Moyers began praying, LBJ said, 'Speak up, Bill. I can't hear you.' Moyers replied, 'I wasn't talking to you, Mr. President.'"

"When we flew back to Austin on Air Force One

when Johnson's presidency was over, he was asked when did he feel he was no longer president, and he said, 'Four seconds after Nixon was sworn in.'"

On President Richard Nixon:
"He always had two roads to take, and he always chose the wrong one."
"I passed President Nixon in the White House on the day he was going to resign, and I asked him how he was doing. He said, 'Pray for me, Helen.'"

On Henry Kissinger:
"A woman ran up to Henry Kissinger and said, 'Oh, Dr. Kissinger. Thank you for saving the world.' He replied, 'You're welcome.'"

On President Gerald Ford:
"Gerald Ford told us on the day he became president, 'Our long national nightmare is over.'"

On First Lady Betty Ford:
"When we asked Betty Ford if she knew her husband was sometimes a bit awkward, bumping his head and so on, she said, 'So what else is new?'"

On President Jimmy Carter:
"Jimmy Carter missed his calling as a minister."
"One time I was barred from covering a Sunday School class taught by Jimmy Carter because 'ladies' were not allowed, and I told them, 'I'm no lady. I'm a reporter.'"

On presidential brother Billy Carter:

"When we asked Billy Carter if he, too, had been born again, he said, 'Once is enough.'"

On Miss Lilian (Carter's mother):

"Miss Lillian said, 'Sometimes when I look at my children, I wish I had remained a virgin.'"

"Once when I was waiting in the doorway for an interview with Miss Lillian, she was finishing an interview with a French reporter. The reporter was repeatedly asking Miss Lillian if she ever told a lie. In exasperation, Miss Lillian finally said, 'Well, sometimes I might tell a little, white lie.' The reporter perked up. Miss Lillian said, 'Remember when you walked in the room, and I told you how beautiful you looked? That's a little, white lie!'"

On President Ronald Reagan:

"When we came back from a trip to the Soviet Union as the Cold War was ending, I asked Ronald Reagan if he thought if he had visited before, he would have found out that the Soviets laughed and cried—that they were human. Reagan said, 'No. They've changed.'"

"There is no doubt there was a Reagan revolution. He moved the country to the right."

On President George H.W. Bush:

"He was a foreign policy president. He saw the Berlin Wall crumble, and the Soviet Union collapse."

On President Bill Clinton:

"There is no doubt he tarnished the Oval Office."

On President George W. Bush:

"George W. Bush is the worst president in history. Yes, I said it."

On President Barack Obama:

"The first black president and I share a birthday. Guess who's older?"

Helen also talked about journalism in her speeches:

"We in the press have a special role since there is no other institution in a democracy that can hold the president accountable."

"We don't go into journalism to win popularity contests."

And in later years, "Everyone with a laptop thinks they're a journalist."

Helen also loved to quote from the fictional 19th Century bartender, Mr. Dooley, who was created by the *Saturday Evening Post* columnist Finley Peter Dunne: "The job of a newspaper is to comfort the afflicted and afflict the comfortable."

Finally, Helen's advice to young people who want to grow up to be president: "If you want to be president, you better decide at the age of 5—and live your life accordingly."

However, not everything associated with Helen's speeches was fun and games. Oftentimes, the problems were caused by travel issues. For instance, Helen was supposed to give a speech at a college in Ohio. Over Helen's objections, the university insisted upon sending its private plane to pick her up. Helen got aboard the small plane and was greeted by a professor, the professor's daughter, and her granddaughter, a child around 8 years old.

The plane took off, and moments later, the pilot appeared in the passenger area. He asked if he could offer anyone a beverage. When everyone declined, he said, "Then it is my moral obligation to let you know we lost some of our wheels upon takeoff, so we might have some trouble landing. We are being diverted to the Columbus airport where they have better safety equipment. If there is a fire, a slide will be opened."

The group sat in silence. Helen said she wondered if she should take her purse with her if they had to go down the slide. She was feeling a bit panicked until she looked at the child on the plane who was calmly reading a book. She thought to herself, "If a kid can be calm, then so can I."

When they came in for landing at the Columbus airport, Helen looked out the plane's window. She saw white foam on the runway, and lots of people wearing fire-proof jumpsuits. There were dozens of fire trucks and ambulances. Luckily, the plane landed safely on its belly. Helen told me, "I don't like private planes."

However, that was not the last time Helen flew on a private plane. She was invited to be the mid-year commencement speaker at a college in the Upper Peninsula of Michigan where my mom sat on the board.

In order to get to the UP, as Michiganders refer to it, Helen had to make a connection in Detroit.

The weather in Michigan was not good, with snow coming down furiously. Helen's connection to the UP was cancelled. To add insult to injury, Helen's checked bag was somehow sent to Japan. My phone lines were burning up with calls from Helen, my mom, and school officials.

Helen was determined to make it to the UP, so a plan was hatched. The school would send its private plane, but Helen had to get to another nearby airport by taxi. Meantime, my mom, who was already in the Upper Peninsula, would buy Helen some clothes to wear to dinner at the university president's house that evening, and under her regalia the next day. My mom's shopping experience resulted in several more phone calls, since apparently the selection to choose from in the small town was not stellar.

Helen got into a cab to get to the airport where the university's plane was set to pick her up. A normally 20-minute ride took nearly three hours, and not because of the snow. The cab driver was lost. I received more calls from everyone involved, with Helen assuring me she would get there. I wondered about the safety of traveling on a small plane when the commercial flight was cancelled due to weather, but Helen was determined.

She eventually made it to the UP, had dinner at the school president's house, and gave a successful graduation speech. When it came time to leave, the university planned to fly my mom and the other board members from the Detroit area home on the school's plane, and Helen was to fly on the commercial flight booked back to Washington with a connection through Detroit.

As they readied to leave the college, Helen asked my mom if she could fly with them on the school's plane to Detroit, and then take the commercial flight to DC. My mom spoke with the pilot who told her it shouldn't be a problem—provided someone was willing to sit in an "unusual" seat for the flight. Determined to get Helen on the plane after all she had been through getting to the UP, my mom told the pilot she would be more than happy to sit in whatever seat was necessary to make it work.

They boarded the plane, and my mom waited to see her "unusual" seat. The pilot strapped a jump seat onto the toilet, and that was where my mom sat for the short flight. At least the bathroom door was tied open.

There were other times when Helen created her own predicaments with speeches.

Helen was always meeting people on planes. One time when she came back from a speech, she told me about a man she sat next to on her flight who was "down on his uppers." By this time, I was representing Helen as her agent, so she asked me if I would mind if she did a speech for this "poor man" who ran a speakers' bureau. I readily agreed, knowing full well it was useless to argue with Helen when she made up her mind about something.

Helen did the speech, and a couple of months later, she had not been paid. Helen asked me to call the man who arranged the speech. I called every other day for a month, trying to find out about Helen's money. I finally told Helen that it seemed she had two choices. She could consider the speech charity, or she could hire an attorney to sue the man. She chose to forget about the payment, and I assumed the issue was off my desk.

A couple of months later, Helen called me quite upset. She said an FBI agent had left her a message, and she was "afraid" to call him back. When Helen was worried, there was no reasoning with her, so when she asked me to return the FBI agent's call, I eventually consented. It was quite a story.

The FBI wanted Helen to testify in a case they were building against the man with the speakers' bureau. He had ripped off dozens of celebrities who had made speeches and were never paid. The FBI became involved when 60 *Minutes* journalist Andy Rooney became one of the speakers' bureau's victims.

After trying and trying to reach the man who had promised him the honorarium, Rooney found out where the man lived. He went to the man's house with a camera crew and knocked on the door with cameras rolling. When the door opened, he said, "I'm Andy Rooney, and I'm here for my money." The man slammed the door in Rooney's face. Andy Rooney reported the crooked behavior to the FBI, and the investigation turned up dozens of similar instances of celebrities making speeches and not being paid. Apparently, the man kept detailed notes on his computer about all of these speeches. He was pocketing all the money the groups thought they were paying to the celebrity speakers.

Helen was distraught over having to testify. One would have thought she was being tried for murder rather than testifying as a witness in the case. My dad and her niece's husband, both practicing attorneys, helped ease Helen's fears, and she made it through her day in court. After it was all over, Helen told me, "I have to stop picking up people and letting them use me." Right. But she never learned.

Books

Helen was a prolific writer, not only as a journalist, but also as the author of six books. Her first book, written in 1975, was *Dateline: White House*. I was only 13 years old when it was published, but I remember being thrilled to receive a signed copy.

I was the agent who represented Helen's other five books. After I narrowed the list of publishers to those that seemed especially interested in Helen's first book, we went to New York to meet with them. Things did not go exactly as expected. Helen got into a heated political argument with one of the acquiring editors. She insulted another publisher with snide comments. However, we were able to generate enough interest to run an auction for the book, which was eventually acquired by Scribner, an imprint of Simon and Schuster.

Helen hired a UPI colleague to help her with the book, and the three of us spent many long nights sitting at Helen's table at Ayesha's trying to pull the information out of Helen to turn it into a book. Looking back, it was fascinating to hear Helen's recollections about the historical ups and downs she covered. But it seemed like a real chore at that time.

The manuscript was finally turned into the publisher, and we all heaved a temporary sigh of relief. That is, until we got the edits back. There was one glaring omission Helen's editor noticed. There was no mention of Helen's late husband, Doug Cornell, any place in the manuscript. Helen dug her heels in, saying she did NOT want to write about Doug; it was her book, she had the right to include or exclude whatever information she chose. The publisher was insistent that Doug be included.

While all this was going on, my dad came to Washington for business and stayed with me. I told him about Helen's stance on her manuscript and asked if he could talk with Helen—who thought my father walked on water. We had lunch at my place with Helen. We were still sitting at the table after finishing our meal, and I gave my dad a pointed look. Finally, he broached the topic. He said, "So, I hear the book is coming along. What are you going to say about Doug?" It was the only time I ever saw Helen lash out at my dad. She screamed, "What in the hell business is it of yours?!?" My father sat in stunned silence. Helen huffed out the door, and my dad commented, "Well, she sure handed me my head on a silver platter." We never understood why Helen was so reluctant to add anything to the book about Doug. Maybe it was simply too painful to recall her loss, but the next day she wrote a few things about him in the manuscript—at least enough to satisfy her publisher.

In 1999, Helen's memoir, *Front Row at the White House,*

was published, and I decided to give her a launch party at Ayesha's. We picked a menu and engaged a local bookstore to sell the books at the event. Helen began to make a guest list that finished with about 100 names, which seemed reasonable to me. By the day of the party, more than 800 of our "closest" friends would attend. Other than costing me eight times more than anticipated, I was happy to see such interest.

I put the arm on friends to help with the party, and everyone seemed to enjoy it. There were friends and colleagues, senators and members of Congress, cabinet members, and TV personalities. We also garnered media coverage, including CNN. They stayed almost the entire time, interviewing the better-known guests. We did have one minor incident when someone from *The National Enquirer* showed up uninvited. Helen insisted he be asked to leave. Luckily, two of our friends helping with the party were off-duty Secret Service agents, so I assigned them the task of evicting the reporter.

Helen signed books for hours and hours, never even taking a bathroom break. The bookstore ran out of books, so they called other stores in the area and picked up their inventory to sell at the party. The volume of books sold set a record for the largest number of books sold "off-site" in the history of the bookstore (at that time). I would say the party was a success.

Helen's next book, *Thanks for the Memories, Mr. President*, was published in 2002. She again asked her (by then former) UPI colleague to help her. There were more long dinners at Ayesha's to get the book written.

This time, Helen's cranky side reared its head during a photo shoot for the cover. The publisher wanted a photo of Helen with the White House in the background, so they hired a photographer. Helen arranged for all of us to be cleared into the White House, but there was a caveat. The White House required the group to be escorted by a White House staffer when we went outside on the grounds.

We all met in the briefing room of the White House, and Helen was waiting. I asked where our escort was in order to get the photo shoot going. Helen said in a snappish way, "How in the hell do I know? Why don't you go ask in the lower Press Office?" With everyone looking at me, I confidently walked to the area adjacent to the briefing room, only to discover nobody knew what I was talking about. They asked to speak to Helen. She refused. Back and forth I went, finally convincing someone to walk us outside.

When the photographer settled on a spot to take the photo, she placed a piece of masking tape on the driveway where she wanted Helen to stand. Helen was having nothing of it. The photographer, with Helen standing right there, said, "Could you please get your client to cooperate?" I pleaded with Helen to "just get it over with and stand in front of the masking tape." Helen eventually did as she was asked.

However, the difficulty did not end there. The photographer began snapping photos and telling Helen to "smile, just a little." Each time the photographer urged Helen to smile, a more and more sour look came across Helen's face. The photographer looked at me, and commanded, "Tell her to smile!" Again, I said to Helen, "Let's just get this over with. Please try to put a smile on your face." I was feeling awkward, not knowing how to get Helen to smile, when the photographer asked me to say something funny to get Helen to laugh. I guess the thought of me as a stand-up comic struck Helen as funny, and the photographer was able to get some shots. I never knew how hard a photo shoot could be.

In 2006, Helen's book, *Watchdogs of Democracy*, was published. By this time, the woman who worked on Helen's previous books was worn out, so Helen hired her friend Maggie Kilgore to take on the task. Helen and Maggie knew one another from their days working at UPI, and Maggie was known for being one of only a handful of women covering the Vietnam War. Maggie lived in California, but she was willing to come to Washington to stay with Helen for an indefinite period of time to get the book done. A former journalist herself, Maggie thought the topic was interesting. However, she had forgotten about how Helen liked to procrastinate and edge up close to deadlines. She also forgot how hot Helen kept her home.

Maggie arrived in the thick heat and humidity that is typical of Washington during the summer. About two weeks or so into her working-stay with Helen, Maggie arrived at my door, dripping wet from sweat. She said, "Can I come in and cool off?" I looked at her, and thought, "This can't be healthy!" I gave her a cold drink, and we chatted. She mentioned the manuscript was not started. I said I would talk with Helen.

Helen assured me she was going to "buckle down and

get to work" on the manuscript. I relayed this to Maggie, who seemed relieved that there was still plenty of time before the book had to be turned into the publisher. A couple of weeks flew by, and the book was still not started. However, Helen had Maggie taking care of other things, and there were plenty of social activities in the evenings.

For instance, Helen had new carpet installed throughout her home. Maggie was in charge of meeting the carpet installers and supervising their work. Maggie also cooked a lot of dinners for the three of us, with Maggie and I doing the grocery shopping. Helen was happily at the White House, doing what she loved best, covering the news of the day. In the evenings when Maggie didn't cook, the three of us went out to dinner, usually with people joining us. Maggie thought a lot of these people were "kooky"—and did not understand why Helen was "wasting her time."

Maggie also pointed out other time-wasters she thought were peculiar. Every Sunday at 9:30 in the morning, the phone would ring. Apparently, a woman who lived in New York got Helen's phone number from the phone book. They would talk about the political issues of the day. After half an hour of speaking, the woman would declare, "That's all I have to say," and hang up. When Maggie asked Helen if the Sunday caller was a friend, Helen said, "I've never met her."

Meantime, the book deadline was quickly approaching and very little was written. Frustrated, Maggie called me to say she could not stay much longer if Helen did not intend to write the book. I said I would talk with Helen again. As usual, Helen said she would get to work.

The next day, Helen called Maggie from work. She said, "I know I promised you I would come right home from the White House so we can work on my book. But we have to go to one more dinner tonight. You're really going to like her." Maggie asked, "Who is it?" Helen replied, "The woman who runs the hot dog stand at the airport."

The deadline was met, but not easily. Helen enlisted help from one of my friends to write a section on bloggers, and I wrote two sections of the book on the FCC and managed news at the White House. I was relatively knowledgeable about the topics I was assigned since I had written lengthy papers on them while in law school, though there had been changes to both areas subsequent to when the papers were written. We were all relieved when I sent the manuscript to the publisher.

Helen's next book was a children's work, *The Great White House Breakout*. Published in 2008 by Dial Books, an imprint of Penguin, it was a collaboration with Chip Bok as the illustrator. Chip is a syndicated editorial, political cartoonist with a conservative slant—not exactly in line with Helen's more liberal-leaning views. However, the book's non-political nature allowed Helen and Chip to get along well.

Because children's picture books rely more heavily on the illustrator than the author, this book was really Chip's project. Chip and his wife, Deb, came to Washington a few times to meet with us over dinner, and Helen was more than agreeable to Chip's approach to the book.

Chip worked hard, and the result was a lively, colorful book for children about a child who was the son of the president. He had a pet cat, and the cat had a mouse friend. The trio was bored with the confines imposed by living at the White House, so they broke out of the mansion to visit some of the popular sites in the nation's capital while the Secret Service frantically searched for the missing boy. It was an adorable book with great potential.

However, the book did not fare as well as expected since Helen fell ill, and she was unable to promote the book with her usual interviews and book signing appearances. I think this came as an extreme disappointment to Chip after his months and months of work, but his heart was in the right place, expressing concern and worry over Helen's health.

As soon as the children's work was turned into the publisher, Helen began thinking about her next book for adults. At the same time, my friend and client, Craig Crawford, was talking to me about writing his next book. I had an idea: a co-authored book by Helen and Craig, two political junkies who mostly saw eye to eye.

I set up a dinner meeting at the Prime Rib, a Washington restaurant on K Street, to discuss the possibilities. The restaurant was one of Helen's favorites, so she readily agreed to the dinner. After discussing the political issues of the day, we eventually got around to talking about topics for the co-authored book.

Helen and Craig were drinking red wine while the conversation was taking place. Suddenly, Craig motioned, and wine went all over the place, including on the robin blue, ultra-suede jacket Helen was wearing. Craig was immediately apologetic, saying he was sorry over and over again. In fact, he felt so terrible that every time he saw Helen for the next month or so, he again repeated his regret over his accident. In typical Helen fashion, when someone made a mistake, she took it all in stride. She said it didn't matter. She would just have the jacket cleaned. We never saw the jacket again.

However, an idea was born for the book at the dinner, ultimately resulting in the 2009 publication by Helen's publisher, Scribner, of *Listen Up, Mr. President*. But there were delays in writing the proposal to show to the publisher because of Helen's illness.

When Helen recovered and the book was published, Craig, Helen, and I had a lot of fun promoting it. We crisscrossed the country for the authors to make joint appearances. There were trips to Florida, New York, and the West Coast. There also were local book events and parties.

One such party was given by the Lebanese ambassador. Helen asked Craig and me to work out the details for the party with the ambassador, who insisted that he meet with someone in person.

When Craig and I met with the ambassador, he seemed primarily focused on the guest list since the embassy entertained frequently, and they knew what they were doing. Helen wanted to include her friends, family, colleagues, and some notable reporters and political types. Craig and I noticed that the ambassador was questioning why certain possible guests with Jewish-sounding names were being invited. He would say things like, "The space cannot hold all these people." But he only mentioned this about Jewish people on the guest list. Craig and I were both more than uncomfortable. When I spoke to Helen about the meeting after it was over, she said, "Tell the ambassador I am not interested in the party if I can't invite my friends." I sent a more "delicately" worded email to the ambassador, and he got the message.

The party was nice, and lots of people showed up. As is typical at book parties, the authors, Helen and Craig, spent the entire evening signing copies of their books. The line for signing was long, so appetizers were served to the people impatiently waiting to have books signed.

When people got up to the table with Helen and Craig, they wanted to linger, take photos, and spend as much time as possible. I tried to keep people moving along so everyone could have their books signed. But there was one individual who could not get enough of Helen, and it was somewhat ironic because of his conservative politics. Congressman Darrell Issa, a Republican from California, seemed delighted to be in Helen's company. He had his book signed, posed for numerous photos with Helen, and stood by her side while she was signing others' books, all the while smiling.

After the party, Craig joked with Helen about it, saying, "How's your good pal, Darrell Issa, doing?" Years later, Representative Issa announced he would not seek re-election when his term was up. Craig sent me an email that read in part, "Did you see that Helen's ole buddy (just kidding) Darrell Issa's bailing out of Congress? He fawned all over her at that embassy event, although he did buy a bunch of books." I emailed Craig back that the same thought had popped into my head when I heard he was not going to run again.

I think this demonstrates that, occasionally, politics can be put aside, after all.

Travels with Helen

Other than weekends at the cabin, Helen rarely took vacations, so our trips for pleasure were memorable, if infrequent. We usually went to New York for the weekend to take in a Broadway show and explore the restaurant scene. On one of these jaunts to the Big Apple, Helen and I took the Delta Shuttle—the last time I took that particular shuttle for a while.

In those days, passengers could show up at the airport, purchase a plane ticket to NYC, and board the next plane. Shuttles left every hour.

Helen and I were at the counter to purchase our tickets when the Delta employee suggested Helen might qualify for a discounted senior ticket if she presented an ID to prove her age. One would have thought the man had asked Helen to fly outside the plane by her reaction. She went ballistic, swearing, and screaming, "How dare you! It's none of your damn business how old I am. What's it to you? How old are *you*?" I tried to interrupt Helen's rant as the Delta employee stood there looking aghast. I said, "Helen, you can get a discounted ticket. Just show him your ID." Helen would hear nothing of it. I purchased my ticket and moved away from the counter. Helen finally joined me.

As we boarded the plane, I was a few steps ahead of Helen when I suddenly heard her shrieking my name. I doubled back to the door of the jetway where Helen was standing. Apparently, she had not purchased a ticket at all, so she was prevented from boarding the airplane by the Delta gate agent. By now, other passengers were recognizing Helen, making matters even worse. She was yelling at the top of her lungs to anyone who would listen about how terribly she had been treated by Delta.

I spoke with the gate agent, who assured me they would hold the plane while I ran back to the counter and purchased a full-price ticket for Helen. When I arrived with the ticket and handed it to Helen, she said, "Did you get the discount?" I didn't answer, but I knew I would not be able to fly the Delta Shuttle for a while for fear of being recognized by the Delta employees!

When we finally got to New York, Helen asked to join me with some friends at a singalong joint. I knew Helen loved to sing, but the bar had an unusually high number of gay men. I wasn't sure Helen was entirely comfortable with this—until the entire crowd in the packed place began chanting her name, over and over again. Helen couldn't resist. She sang her heart out to the delight of the other patrons.

Another short trip was to Ocean City, Maryland. Helen knew a couple who threw her a weekend-long birthday celebration at the hotel, The Carousel. Other than a friend and I who drove Helen to the hotel where the activities were taking place, there were not many of

Helen's friends in attendance. Instead, all of the hosting couple's large, extended family and friends were there. Helen originally knew the hosts because the husband had been a janitor in the White House, and, I suspected, a source for Helen. His wife was a rotund, bossy woman who spoke as though she had her mouth wired shut, with her lips barely moving. Helen objected to how "programmed" the weekend was, and peoples' constant need for Helen to pose for pictures with the other guests. None of us had a bad time, but we all agreed that we never needed to repeat the weekend.

The only time Helen ever took off more than a few days for a vacation was a trip we took with The Ladies. My family owned a resort in Traverse City, Michigan, a beautiful location on a bay off Lake Michigan in the "little finger" of the mitten-shaped state. One evening when I was having dinner with The Ladies, they decided they would like to see the resort they had heard so much about, and they also decided Helen's sisters and my grandmother could meet us there. Traverse City is about a four-hour drive from the Detroit area where Helen's family and Me-mama lived.

My parents made arrangements for gratis accommodations at the resort, and I was advised to sign my name for meals and any other activities we did on the resort property. I rented a large van to haul everyone around.

Helen and I were going to meet The Ladies at the airport on the day of the trip. At dinner with Helen the evening before, she said, "I'll call a cab to take us to National (airport) in the morning, so I'll meet you in the lobby at 5 a.m." Our flight didn't leave until around 9 a.m., and the airport was only 10 to 15 minutes from our condo building. I thought Helen was joking.

Apparently, it was not a joke. At 5 a.m. the following morning, the phone ringing woke me from a sound sleep. When I answered, Helen said, "The cab is here, so come down as soon as you can." I am quick in the morning, but there was no way I could shower and dress while the taxi waited. I told Helen I would meet her at the airport.

When I arrived at the airport in plenty of time for our flight, Fran told me Helen was quite upset with me. She was correct. Helen refused to speak to me until we finally made it to northern Michigan, despite the fact that we sat next to each other on the flight from DC to Detroit, and on our connection from Detroit to Traverse City.

When we met up with Helen's sisters and Me-mama at the resort, all of the hugging and kissing broke Helen's foul mood. But that was not the last we saw of her temper. After checking in and unpacking, we agreed to meet in the lobby of the main part of the hotel. I never realized how difficult it would be to get a bunch of older women to decide what to do. I suggested everyone could do whatever they wanted, and we could meet for a drink before dinner. I suddenly became the enemy.

Fran wanted to take out one of the sailboats—with me. Dorothy O wanted to take a tour of the main commercial kitchen—with me. One of Helen's sisters wanted to read by one of the swimming pools—with me. Helen wanted to find a restaurant that served smelt, a small, bony fish indigenous to the area. The only accommodating, rational women in the group were Me-mama and her friend, Helen's sister Issy. They kept the peace by explaining the obvious: I could not be in all these places at the same time.

Somehow, we settled on a plan for the day with a promise to Helen that we would eat at a smelt-serving restaurant the next day.

Later, I walked by myself through the bar in the lobby while the women rested before dinner. A bartender who had worked at the resort for years waved me over. She said, "I thought I saw you earlier, but then I thought it couldn't have been you since all these blue-haired women were walking with you." I just looked at the bartender and gave her an exasperated smile.

The next day, I loaded everyone into the rental van for shopping and a lunch of smelt in Leland, a nearby town on Lake Michigan. The Ladies got into a political argument on the way there, but everyone enjoyed lunch. Neither Me-mama nor I had smelt since we knew one ate the entire fish, bones and all, but everyone else seemed up for the adventure of the regional cuisine.

After lunch we planned to shop in the quaint, waterside town. Because there were so many of us, I thought we should set an approximate time to meet by the parked van. This is when Helen's foul mood returned from out of nowhere and over nothing. She went berserk, and even directed the "f-bomb" at me repeatedly. To this day, I do not know what she was upset about. Thankfully, the situation was resolved when others in the group began to walk away saying,

"See you back at the van." Me-mama, Issy, and I spent the rest of the afternoon poking around the shops and sitting by the water.

Everyone appeared back at the van, and not a word was uttered about Helen's earlier meltdown. The rest of the trip was pleasant enough, and there were no more angry scenes.

As Helen got older, I frequently traveled with her for speaking engagements, interviews, and book signings. Helen needed more help with carrying her many bags, most of which she carried on the plane with her. She used to joke that she was a bag lady, and when I traveled with Helen, I knew what she meant. She also did not like the "newer" things in hotel rooms such as alarm clocks, television remotes, and heat or air conditioning controls. We would no sooner get into our rooms when Helen would call me to come to her room to adjust the temperature or show her how to turn the TV on, usually to CNN. She liked me to set the alarm clock in the room, though she always asked the hotel for a wakeup call to be sure she got up on time.

I remember Helen telling me about when she went on President Nixon's breakthrough trip to China in 1972. As usual, Helen requested a wakeup call at the hotel they stayed at. When the call came in the morning, Helen answered the phone, and a Chinese person would shout in English, "Wake up!" before hanging up. I think Helen preferred this since it was a live human being rather than the recordings that had become so common in all hotels.

We traveled the country together, up and down the

coasts, and throughout the middle. Helen could be difficult going through security in airports, especially subsequent to the 9/11 tragedy that led to increasing security measures.

I remember one time when Helen did a speech and book signing in Oklahoma City. Our flight was quite early, and, as she had repeatedly made clear, she liked to be at the airport at least three hours before her flight was scheduled to take off. She also liked to burn the midnight oil, so I was feeling exhausted when we were picked up from our hotel to go to the airport at 4:30 a.m.

The security line at the airport was long, especially given the early hour. We made our way in the maze of the line, guided by the usual ropes and stanchions. All of a sudden, Helen began quietly saying something. I didn't need to tell her to speak up, because soon I could hear her quite clearly. Her voice grew louder and louder as she became increasingly agitated, all the while repeating, "This is Pavlovian! This is Pavlovian!" I could hear whispers from other people in the security line saying, "That's Helen Thomas!" I tried to calm Helen by telling her we were almost to the front, but she would have nothing of it. She continued her rant, eventually chiding another passenger when he asked her to "cool it." After Helen let the poor man have it, shouting directly at him, the man responded with, "This is not the White House, so even Helen Thomas has to wait in line!"

When we finally could see the conveyer belt for our belongings to be put through security, I mentioned to Helen she would need to take off her shoes. By her reaction, one would have thought I was requesting her to take off all her clothes. She said, "I am NOT going to take off my shoes! I am NOT! Not now or ever!"

Helen grew more hysterical as we approached the front of the queue—still wearing her shoes. By this time, it felt as though everyone in the airport was watching this scene with interest. I calmly explained to Helen that if she walked through the security device with her shoes on, I was certain she would be given a pat-down by the TSA. Helen refused to listen.

I walked through security first, and then I turned to look at what was going to happen with Helen still wearing her shoes. The TSA agent politely said, "You will have to remove your shoes." Ignoring the directive, Helen proceeded through with her shoes on. Someone from the never-ending line shouted, "Just take off your damn shoes so we all can get through security, Helen!"

Three TSA agents surrounded Helen, with her screaming at them, "You can't make me take off my shoes!" A female TSA agent told Helen to come with her. Helen refused, and began shouting my name. I approached the gathering of people, not sure what I could—or should—do. The female agent said they might have to arrest my "friend" since she was "unruly and uncooperative." So, I directed my comments to Helen, "Do you want to be arrested? I told you if you didn't take off your shoes like EVERYBODY is required to do, they would pat you down. Now, let them do their jobs so we don't miss our plane."

I guess Helen was shocked I couldn't prevent the TSA pat-down, so she reluctantly allowed herself to be escorted to a private area where I overheard screams coming from Helen from behind the screen. When it was over, Helen would not speak to me. In fact, she did not talk to me the entire flight. We got in a cab after landing, and as she was exiting the cab at the White House, Helen said, "It was a nice trip." I knew that was her way of apologizing.

We were good with all the other airports' security until a trip to Wisconsin. The group Helen spoke to had given her a box of cheese. She did not open it but put it in one of her carry-on bags. After Helen's bags went through the security X-ray machine, a TSA agent said one of the bags contained a weapon. Perplexed, and with a slightly hostile tone, Helen told him that was "bullshit," since she was not carrying a gun, didn't believe in guns, and would never carry a gun with her.

The TSA agent proceeded to open the box of cheese Helen was given, and there, inside the box, was a small, plastic knife. The TSA offered the box back to Helen, minus the little knife. Crisis averted. As Helen turned to walk toward the gate, the TSA agent yelled, "I know who you are. Good to see you, Secretary Albright." He thought Helen was the first female secretary of state, Madeleine Albright, making the entire episode all the more ridiculous in Helen's mind. The incident was mentioned in local news reports, and the group that gave Helen the box of cheese sent the article with their apologies.

At times, there were bigger issues than airport security. There were occasionally real, personal security issues. Helen and another of my clients, a member of

Congress, decided to do a number of joint appearances. I traveled with Helen to the representative's district. A mutual friend who lived in the area volunteered to drive us around in a rented van so we would all more easily fit. The friend was an off-duty Secret Service agent, which turned out to be a good thing.

After a book signing at a local bookstore, we piled into the van to head to another event at a college when my cell phone rang. It was our contact from the college, calling to inform me they had received death threats aimed at both authors. I told her I would get back to her. Hesitantly, I relayed the message to the gang in the van. Everyone agreed the show must go on, so our driver, the off-duty Secret Service agent, coordinated with the local police to be sure everyone was protected, and security was tight.

We arrived on the campus to a large police presence, but everyone was still on edge. The event was in a good-sized auditorium with a stage in the front. The theatre-style seating was full. My clients and I went backstage with the school contact while our Secret Service friend talked with the police and did security checks.

The program went off without a hitch, with someone from the college leading a discussion with Helen and the member of Congress on the stage. I waited nervously backstage.

At the conclusion of the program, two tables were set up on the stage for the book signing: one for the bookseller and the other for the authors. The authors' table was off to one side of the stage, and the line of people eagerly awaiting getting their books signed seemed to grow exponentially. I walked up and down the line to be sure everyone had filled out a Post-it indicating to whom they wanted their books inscribed.

All of a sudden, I heard Helen and the member of Congress screaming my name in unison. I glanced their way and saw a man standing behind the table where the two authors were sitting. With adrenaline pushing me, I approached the table and said, "Excuse me, sir. Can you please stay in front of the table?" Motioning to the extensive line of people, I continued, "If you would like to have a book signed, the line is over here."

The man aggressively came from behind the table and moved toward me. Instinctively, I backed up to avoid him. But he grabbed me and threw me against the back wall. I yelled for our Secret Service friend, who seemingly came to my rescue from out of nowhere. I was impressed by how quickly the agent got the man in some type of a hold, escorted him off the stage and handed him over to the police.

Meantime, with the disruption over, the two authors went back to signing copies of their books. We learned later that the man had a police record, and that he appeared to be mentally ill. We were all grateful no one was hurt, but we were glad to get off that college campus, nonetheless.

When there weren't security issues to worry about, there were always other issues of concern. Sometimes these issues were unbelievably perplexing, like a trip to New York for Helen to appear on ABC's *Good Morning America.*

Helen and I were planning on going up to New York

for her to do the show when a friend decided to join us. Because we had to be at the studio early in the morning, we traveled the day before, early enough to eat dinner in the Big Apple. We checked into a lovely two-bedroom suite at our hotel. Our friend traveling with us agreed to share a room with me, and Helen would have her own room.

After surveying our suite, we grabbed a cab and headed to the agreed-upon restaurant, a recommendation by people we knew living in New York. Upon entering the restaurant, Helen was immediately recognized by the owner. He began fawning all over Helen, offering to serve his best dishes. We were stuffed, but the meal was not complete without dessert.

The owner brought to our table a Lazy Susan turntable loaded with one of each of the desserts on the menu. We had fun spinning the turntable and trying a bite of everything. Somewhere in the middle of our dessert tasting, Helen managed to get various food particles all over the dress she wore, including a long stain of chocolate fudge. She was a mess, but nobody cared—and Helen didn't seem to notice.

We went back to our hotel and fell into bed, feeling more than satisfied. The following morning, our friend went into our suite's kitchen with Helen to make coffee while I tried to grab five more minutes of shuteye. I still must have been tired since I dozed off again.

I woke to my friend shaking me. She was frantically whispering something, but I couldn't quite make out what she was saying in my grogginess. I asked her to repeat herself. In a barely audible whisper so as not to let Helen hear, she explained, "Helen is wearing the dress from last night!" Not recalling the chocolate stains, I responded, "So?" My friend said, "We can't let her go on national TV with that huge chocolate stain! Get up and tell her to wear something different! Now!"

I jumped out of bed and went into the living room. Helen was sitting there, reading a newspaper, drinking coffee—and wearing the stained dress. In as chipper a voice as I could muster, I asked, "So, what are you going to wear for GMA?" Helen looked up, "I thought I would just wear this." In my most delicate tone, I said, "You can't wear a dress with a huge chocolate stain on TV. What else did you bring?" My heart sank when Helen told me she did not bring anything else. At this point, we were only about an hour away from being picked up.

Our friend emerged from the bedroom. We looked at each other, and she mouthed the words, "Who forgets clothes when they are going to be on TV?" Helen continued reading her newspaper as though she didn't have a care in the world, but she finally offered, "I have a sweater with me." I asked to see it. We shoved Helen's arms into the sweater, buttoning it to the top to cover the big chocolate mess and some other food particles from our dessert the previous night. She looked a little silly, but it was certainly a better look than what the sweater hid.

Looking back, a food-stained dress was a minor issue. In early May of 2008, Helen was supposed to speak and sign books at a theatre in Delaware. Because Helen had friends who lived near the theatre, we were to leave in the morning to have time to have lunch with her friends at their home.

A limousine provided by the theatre picked us up in the morning. It was uncharacteristic of Helen to need to stop to use the bathroom, but this time we made several stops for her. I thought she might not be feeling well, but Helen's health was never a good topic, so I kept my thoughts to myself.

Years before, I got a glimpse into how doctor-phobic Helen was when she asked to accompany me on a weekend trip that I was taking to visit a friend in New York—whose father was an ophthalmologist. Helen knew my friend and her parents, but it surprised me that she wanted to tag along. She specifically requested we get together with my friend's parents, but I did not know why. I knew they enjoyed each other's company, but Helen had never asked to come with me on any previous visits.

The ophthalmologist and his wife had us over for lunch, and while we were eating, Helen asked if she could have her eyes checked. The doctor had a small office in his home with the necessary equipment. When the doctor reappeared—without Helen—after checking her eyes, he said he thought Helen needed me. She was hysterical because the doctor found she had cataracts that needed to be removed. Helen cried and cried, and continued bawling, even on the shuttle back to Washington.

Helen immediately asked to use the restroom when we arrived at her Delaware friends' house. She was in there a long time. Her friends asked me if she was okay, but somehow, I managed to change the topic. There was a delicious lunch prepared, but Helen did not eat anything, instead telling our hosts she ate too much in the car for breakfast. She had not eaten a thing on the ride there, and I became more concerned. Helen used their bathroom frequently.

We made it to the theatre, where there was a large crowd of people waiting to hear Helen speak. She asked for the ladies' room when we arrived, and I followed her. I was grateful we were the only people in the bathroom so I could talk with Helen privately. I asked Helen if she was feeling okay, and she snapped at me, "Why would you ask me that? I am fine!" I took a deep breath as we headed to the backstage area of the theatre.

Helen got through her speech and a Q&A, but I thought she was less energetic than usual with her delivery. She *did* enthusiastically greet audience members that included former White House Press Secretary Jim Brady and his wife, Sarah. Jim was severely wounded during the assassination attempt on President Ronald Reagan, and his wife, Sarah, had become a champion of gun control. Helen signed books, and then there was a reception at a restaurant afterward for VIP friends of the theatre. Before we left the theatre, Helen wanted to use the bathroom.

When we arrived at the restaurant, Helen again asked to use the ladies' room, and I again accompanied her. I inquired how she was feeling, and she bit my head off, so I decided to drop the issue until we were headed back to Washington.

There were voluminous amounts of appetizers at the

reception, so I picked out a few I thought Helen would like and brought a small plate over to her where she was seated, holding court with her fans. She set the plate aside and never touched the food. I thought her color did not look good, but I did not want to risk creating a scene in front of the reception attendees.

Several other people brought heaping plates of food to Helen, but she passed on all of them. As the reception neared its end, the restaurant owner, observing Helen had not eaten, offered to pack up some of the food to take with us in the limousine ride home. Helen said it was not necessary, but they made large doggy bags anyway. I reluctantly took the bags, thanked the owner and restaurant employees for their kindness, and feared Helen's reaction.

As soon as we were in the limo, Helen said, "Throw that food away! I am not hungry." I gently responded with, "You haven't eaten anything all day. Do you feel sick to your stomach? What's wrong?" Helen yelled at me, "STOP ASKING IF I FEEL OKAY! I already told you that I am fine." We rode the rest of the way in silence, with Helen dozing off every so often.

When we finally arrived home, I walked Helen to her door and told her to call me if she needed anything. I was extremely worried about her, and I knew something was not right. I spoke to her the following day, but there was no discussion about her health.

Illness Strikes Helen

A few days after our trip to Delaware, Helen was scheduled to deliver a college commencement address. She knew I would not be able to go with her since I was committed to be with another client who had been the ambassador to Madagascar. We had arranged for her to sign books at the Madagascar embassy for Embassy Row's annual open house. A friend who owned a bookstore in New York was coming to Washington to handle the book sales for the signing at the all-day event.

I thought about cancelling my commitment at the embassy so I could travel with Helen, but when I spoke with her, she sounded more like herself. I went to the embassy, and Helen went to her speech alone. I would regret not accompanying Helen.

It was already hot and humid in Washington on this early May day, and the embassy did not seem to have air conditioning, or at least it was not on. All of us sweated our way through the book signing, and when it was over, the author, the bookseller, the bookseller's son (who had made the trip from New York to help his mom), and I decided to grab a bite to eat. The temperature had dropped outside, and it was pleasant, so we went to a restaurant with outdoor seating: Helen's hangout, Ayesha's.

While the others perused the menu I knew well, I decided to check my voicemail. I had my cell phone off at the embassy in an effort to not bother the hordes of people who came through the embassy. Because it was a Saturday, I did not expect anything significant. However, I could not have been more wrong.

I received a message from the husband of one of Helen's nieces. He said Helen had collapsed at the college commencement address and was rushed to a local hospital. I immediately returned the call without even telling my dinner companions what was going on. I did not learn much more, other than that Helen's nieces were on their way to the hospital in Pennsylvania near the college where Helen was speaking.

My heart stopped. Why had I not pressed Helen to go to a doctor when I knew something was dreadfully wrong? I shared my concern with my dinner companions and somehow got through the meal.

When I got home, I called Helen's niece's husband to see if he had an update, and then I called Helen's closest friends, The Ladies. They were all panicked, and I promised to let them know when I knew more.

I later learned Helen was in critical condition and required surgery. After the doctors at the hospital in Pennsylvania got Helen stabilized, she was transported to Georgetown University Hospital in Washington so she could be close to home.

Apparently, Helen had undiagnosed diverticulitis that blew a hole in her large intestine, and it could only be repaired through surgery. This involved removing part of the infected colon where pouches had formed and ruptured, emptying poison into Helen's abdominal cavity. It was serious, and the outcome did not look good.

The surgery was partially successful. The part of the colon the doctors removed was so extensive that Helen ended up with a colostomy bag. I cried when I found this out, since I knew Helen would not be happy. At least she was still alive, but barely. The medical team put Helen in a medically induced coma to allow her body to heal, though they were not sure she would make it.

I felt helpless. I talked obsessively with doctor friends about possible outcomes. Some were comforting, others were not. They all agreed on one point: nobody really knew what might happen.

There are mixed messages about whether people in comas can hear or feel visitors. On the chance that Helen was able to hear me, I visited her in her private ICU room at Georgetown University Hospital almost every day. Before entering the room, I had to dress like I was a part of her medical team due to concerns over further infection. I donned a gown and booties to cover my shoes and rigorously washed my hands before putting on latex gloves. On the way out, there was a container to place the clothes coverings to be disposed of by the hospital staff.

I spoke to Helen and held her hand. I told her I loved her, and I asked her to fight. I discussed politics, and

I told her about my work. I told her The Ladies were waiting to have dinner with her. I felt ridiculous. It was like talking to a wall, but I was hopeful that my talking to Helen might somehow make a difference in her recovery. I hoped she knew how much I rooted for her.

Weeks went by. It was touch and go. Things looked bleak some days. There were more life-saving medical procedures due to setbacks. Other days were more positive. I continued my daily treks to the hospital. I occasionally coordinated with Helen's nieces to meet there.

Helen's family and I were her only visitors while she was in the coma. As if this period of time wasn't tough enough, adding to the difficulty was a request by Helen's family that I not reveal Helen's illness to anyone except a short list of people. That list included my mom and dad, a couple of my closest friends, and Helen's closest friends, The Ladies, who were all still alive. I told others about Helen, but I tried to exercise good judgment about who should know and made every effort to respect Helen's family's wishes.

However, there was the business side of Helen's life, and I was deeply involved since I was her agent. When I asked Helen's family what I should tell everyone, I was told to say she was on vacation. This might work with some people, but not others. Besides, even Helen's acquaintances knew she rarely took vacations. And that wouldn't solve the problem of Helen's business commitments.

For instance, I could not tell organizations that had signed contracts for Helen to speak that she decided to go on vacation. I simply told them that Helen was not able to appear due to unforeseen circumstances, and I refunded the deposits. Some demanded to know what the reason was and became extremely irate. I apologized profusely, offered to find another speaker, and apologized again. A couple of groups threatened to sue me. A couple of people slammed the phone down on me. But I did not reveal Helen's serious illness.

Scheduled interviews were somewhat easier to cancel. When I told the media that Helen would be unable to do the interviews, most were accommodating and simply asked when she could reschedule. I told everyone to contact me again in a month or so. I felt a twinge of guilt, since I didn't know if Helen would even be alive in the next month.

However, the most guilt I felt was when people began calling me to see if I knew where Helen was. Calls came from everywhere and everyone. Former colleagues called. Helen's friends called. Perfect strangers to me called after getting my number from someone who knew my relationship with Helen. I told almost all of these people that Helen was on vacation, as I had been instructed to say. Complicating this lie was the fact that these people knew that Helen rarely, if ever, took a vacation. This fact led some to question me about what was really going on.

I was an emotional wreck over Helen's life-or-death situation, plus the business-related issues, and all the people continuously upset with me or questioning my veracity. I focused on my work as an escape from life's woes.

I was sitting at my desk in my office one day when the phone rang. It was a nurse from Georgetown University Hospital. He told me Helen had been brought out of her coma, and she was asking for me. I dropped what I was doing and raced over to the hospital, feeling somewhat anxious since I did not know what to expect.

I walked into Helen's room. She was alert, but she couldn't speak because she still had a tracheal tube to help her breathe. When Helen saw me, a gigantic smile appeared on her face, and I held back tears of joy. Helen had a pad of paper and pen to write notes. The first note she wrote to me was, "How are you?" I thought it was so kind to ask how I was doing after all she had been through.

In a subsequent note, Helen asked me to turn on CNN. I thought this was an excellent sign that Helen was going to recover, but I still went out to the nearby nurses' station to ask if it was okay to turn on the TV. Much to my surprise, I was told it would be all right, but to raise Helen's bed slowly. I wished someone else had volunteered to raise the bed for Helen since I did not know what I was doing. I managed somehow, and before long, Helen and I were watching CNN together.

This was during Barack Obama's first run for the Presidency, and when Helen became ill, Hillary Clinton had been running against him in the primaries. Clinton had dropped out of the race while Helen was in the coma. After viewing CNN for a while, Helen got a confused look on her face, and wrote, "Where's Hillary?" I explained that while Helen was "asleep," Hillary had dropped out of the race. Helen wrote,

"Maybe one day we will see a woman as president, but it's not going to be easy." That was when I knew Helen was back with us!

However, the day was not without issues. As Helen watched CNN, soaking in all the news and catching up on what she had missed, she began looking around her room. Suddenly, Helen made an angry face, and she wrote furiously, "What are those Jesus pictures doing on the walls?" One of her relatives visiting from Michigan had taped numerous photos of Jesus on the walls of her ICU room. I could tell Helen was agitated, and I knew she was never a fan of organized religion, feeling it was the root cause of many of the worldwide conflicts throughout history. I shrugged, and I told her I didn't know what the pictures were doing on the walls. She wrote, "Take them down!"

Just as I was contemplating how to respond, a nurse showed up with a glass of orange juice with a straw. Helen shoved the nurse's hand away, and wrote, "Now!" The nurse looked at me, and said, "If she doesn't want to drink this, we can always put the feeding tube back in." I thought this was a little much, given what Helen had been through, but I knew I needed to encourage her to drink. I coaxed Helen, but she refused to even take a sip. I nearly fell over laughing when Helen wrote, "Cannot drink with Jesus pictures on walls." I took down the pictures, and Helen happily drank the juice.

I was feeling optimistic that Helen seemed so much like herself until she wrote a note asking if I had a car with me. When I replied affirmatively, Helen began writing again. She said, "Get me out of here! You have to help me escape." I initially thought she was joking, but it quickly became clear to me that Helen was quite serious. She wrote fast and furious notes, pleading with me to help her escape. I didn't know what to do. I told her she was going to get better, and she would be discharged from the hospital when the doctors thought it was safe for her to leave. None of my answers were acceptable. Helen's notes became heart wrenching. She said, "You don't care about me, or you would help me escape. I hate you!" Somehow, I got her off the topic of escaping, but this was not the last of it.

Helen improved physically over the next few days, but her mental state was not good. She got the tracheal tube out, so she was able to communicate verbally, but much of the communication revolved around asking friends and family to help her escape. When a mutual friend (one of the few people who knew about Helen's illness) visited with me, Helen started in again, demanding she be given a ride to "escape from the horrible people that are holding me against my will."

The hospital sent a psychiatrist to talk with her, but Helen insisted she did not need to speak to anyone—she just needed to "get the hell out of here." The doctors were privately reassuring, telling us they were fairly certain this state of mind was temporary. They diagnosed it as ICU Syndrome or Psychosis, which is caused by a patient being in the intensive care unit for a prolonged period of time. The psychosis causes anxiety, paranoia, and unusual behavior, but it is usually temporary.

In addition to Helen's ICU Syndrome, she refused

to eat. Never a particularly large woman, Helen was looking skeletal, and this was alarming. A friend and I plotted ways to get Helen to eat. We asked her if anything sounded appealing. She said, "Watermelon." We brought her watermelon. Helen said, "Spaghetti." We brought her spaghetti that my friend lovingly cooked from scratch. We brought Helen some of her favorites from Ayesha's, her preferred restaurant. While she did not each much, at least she was eating something and gaining back her strength.

It was a good day when Helen was finally moved out of ICU to an intermediate care floor in the hospital. She was getting better and now was curious about what happened to her. Helen never liked discussing medical issues, especially about herself, but she wanted the straight truth. One day when I was visiting, she asked me if I would tell her the truth. When I inquired, "About what?" she said, "About whether I will ever be able to resume my life and work again." Even though I was not certain, I said, "Absolutely. You will cover the White House again." Helen smiled at the thought.

However, the toughest part of the conversation was when Helen asked if I knew about her colostomy bag. I acknowledged I knew, and she quietly said, "I never wanted that." I said, "I know." My heart was breaking for her, but I knew she could—and would—handle the situation.

Helen's health improved incrementally, and she eventually grew strong enough to be moved to a rehabilitation facility. I knew Helen was getting better because her cranky side began to show. She was obstinate and uncooperative with the nurses and health aides, and she hated the food at the rehab center. When food was delivered, she would say things like, "What is this? It smells like dog food." So, my friend and I resumed our catering business, periodically bringing Helen food she liked.

By this time, word had gotten out that Helen was in rehab, and I was glad. Friends came for visits, and it lifted Helen's spirits. We even celebrated Helen's birthday in her rehab room. Jan Smith, a TV reporter and wife of ABC newsman Sam Donaldson, brought a cake, and a small group of friends and family gathered for the celebration. It was low-key, but a nice acknowledgement of Helen's special day, and I think everyone was grateful Helen was still with us.

However, Helen was still not well enough to do many of the necessary daily activities, and she could not walk. It was frustrating for her, especially since she had been so independent. I knew Helen would overcome the situation, and get out of rehab, though. She had an iron will, and she was not one to back down when she wanted or needed something.

Meantime, when Helen became ill, HBO was making a documentary on Helen's life, and she always enjoyed being in front of the camera, though she never admitted it.

TV and Films

Helen always enjoyed acting, singing, and being onstage, so she was thrilled when we got an offer for her to play herself in a cameo appearance in the 1993 political comedy, *Dave*, starring Kevin Kline and Sigourney Weaver. In the film, when the president has a stroke while having sex with an aide and slips into a coma, a temp agency owner who looks like the president is asked to step in to secretly act as commander-in-chief.

Helen played herself in the movie, questioning the presidential double at a press conference in the briefing room when he makes a bold announcement. Helen practiced her one line repeatedly, using different inflections to find just the right delivery.

Having perfected the line to her satisfaction, she asked me to find out what she should wear for her performance, and word came back that Helen should dress as she would for an actual news conference. So, Helen set out for Hollywood with one of her signature red dresses. Wearing red came about during the Reagan era when all the reporters decided to wear red to a press conference since it was First Lady Nancy Reagan's favorite color, and the White House press corps believed they would have a shot at being called on. Helen subsequently became identified with her red dress.

It took about 12 hours to complete Helen's two-minute scene, but she did have her own dressing room. However, when she appeared on the set in her red dress, the wardrobe person asked, "What are you wearing?" Helen explained she was told to dress how she would at a real presidential press conference, so she was wearing a red dress, something with which she had become identified. The wardrobe person told Helen her dress would not work and handed her a drab, gray dress to wear. When Helen asked for an explanation, the wardrobe person told her a red dress might "upstage" the real stars of the film. Helen wore the dress provided.

Helen's scene that made the final cut in the movie shows her rolling her eyes at the "president's" grandiose announcements for bettering the country. Afterward, when people asked Helen if she was told to roll her eyes, she explained that it was just a "natural reaction"—having heard so many similar promises from the real presidents over the years.

Helen was again asked to play herself in Steven Soderbergh's 2000 thriller, *Traffic*, starring Michael Douglas. The plot revolved around drug trafficking and the United States' war on drugs.

The day of Helen's shoot, we arrived at the house in Georgetown that had been rented for the film and walked up the steep, circular driveway. At the top of the driveway, we ran into a friend who was waiting to be an extra in the movie. She complained she had been waiting hours, and she was curious to find out what we were doing there. When I told her Helen had a cameo playing herself at a cocktail party where the "president" was introducing his newest cabinet member, the friend exclaimed, "Does Helen have a speaking role? Will you get to meet Michael Douglas?" To which Helen responded, "Of course," as she strode into the house. I shrugged my shoulders and followed Helen into the house.

The crew was finishing shooting another scene, so Helen and I waited on a couch—and waited and waited. Just as we were growing impatient, Michael Douglas appeared and sat with us, exchanging compliments with Helen. Later, Helen would comment, "If you have to wait, Michael Douglas is good company." Even with my limited celebrity knowledge I knew who he was, and while I was not star struck as I would have been with, say, John F. Kennedy, he was very nice to us.

When it was finally time for Helen's scene, we all moved to the next room for one take after another. Hours later, as we were leaving the house, we noted that our friend was still waiting to see if she would be picked as an extra for the film.

After a whole day spent on Helen's scene, it ended up on the cutting room floor, much to Helen's annoyance. But after the long day of the shoot, we went out to dinner with a friend of ours, who met us at the Georgetown house in hopes of meeting Michael Douglas. Sadly, she never met the actor, but we had quite an adventure at dinner.

Because we were in Georgetown, we decided to stay

in the same area of town. After stopping for a drink at the Four Seasons hotel, we walked across the street, intending to dine at La Chaumiere, one of Helen's favorite restaurants. As we were passing by a newly opened place next door, the chef was outside on the sidewalk, and he recognized Helen. He begged us to try his Italian food, and when he said the meal would be "on the house," we agreed to eat there. Course after course of gourmet Italian food was served. However, some of the food wasn't familiar to our friend. This culminated in her wrapping the linguini with black, squid ink in her cloth napkin, and putting it in her oversized handbag so the chef wouldn't know she didn't eat it. After the long dinner was over, we asked our friend to call to let us know she got home okay. When my phone rang, she said, "I am starving, so I'm having a bowl of cereal. Then I'm going to clean the squid ink out of my purse!" So much for gourmet Italian food.

There also were a variety of TV pieces done on Helen's life and career. For instance, the CBS newsmagazine program 60 Minutes did a piece. They shot the one-on-one interview in Helen's condo. This was the last time I remember Helen allowing cameras in her home because the cables left black marks on her white carpeting, but she enjoyed the accolades that came with the territory after the segment aired nonetheless.

A&E also produced an hour-long biography about Helen, and the production created a number of "issues" for me. The producer met with us and expressed interest in interviewing Helen's friends, family, and colleagues, in addition to interviewing Helen. It was decided the interviews of the others would take place first, and then they would interview Helen.

Helen compiled a list of people for me to contact for A&E, including her family members. But Helen specifically asked me not to let one of her family members do an interview for fear of what she might say. It was not about me, nor were these my family, so I told Helen I understood.

Coordinating with the producer, I called everyone to schedule the interviews. The interviews would occur in three cities: Washington DC, New York, and Detroit. Everything was going well until A&E made their trip to Detroit to interview Helen's family there.

That evening, I met Helen for dinner, and she blew her stack at me: "What in the hell do you think you're doing? You have created a rift in my family, and I am not going to stand for it!" I gave her a perplexed look, as I really had no clue what she was referring to. She went on, "You hurt my family's feelings. I will not do the interviews for this unless A&E interviews ALL of my family!"

As it turned out, despite following Helen's explicit directive to be sure one of her family members was NOT interviewed, that individual found out about the others in the family being interviewed, and the relative called Helen to ask why they were not included. Apparently, the situation was all my fault.

However, the bigger issue was that Helen dug in her heels, telling me she would not do the one-on-one interviews with A&E unless they went back to Detroit to interview ALL members of her family, specifically the one Helen had originally told me should not be included in the project. While Helen never explicitly denied this initial request, she did not acknowledge it, either.

Caught between a rock and a hard place, I phoned the producer to inform him of the situation, and to say he was upset would be understatement. He explained they had already been to Detroit, followed Helen's wishes, and it was not in the budget to return to Detroit. I pointed out that Helen was unlikely to cooperate any further, including sitting for the interviews herself.

I ended up going up to New York to meet with the producer face-to-face at his request. He showed me the edited interviews with those who had been interviewed thus far, and asked, "Where would you suggest we fit in another person?" I knew this was a rhetorical question, but I also knew I wanted to save the project.

All of a sudden, an idea popped into my head which I relayed to the producer. I knew that A&E was at least partially owned by ABC (the network) because the contract was done between Helen and ABC. So why not have someone from the ABC affiliate in Detroit conduct the interview with the family member in question? When the producer told me this was a possibility, I was hopeful.

The next day when I was back in my office in DC, the producer called me to have the interview set up with the Detroit ABC affiliate. I relayed the good news to Helen, and I thought the project was back on track. That is until I received a call from the producer a couple of days later asking me to come to New York again.

The purpose of the trip was to let me see the outcome of the interview—which in the producer's opinion was not useable. I had to agree that there was not much that even Helen would have wanted included in the final piece. I stepped out of the producer's office to call Helen. She was insistent that something had to be used.

The producer and I reconvened over dinner with both of us repeating over and over again, "What are we going to do?" But I had another idea. Helen had not asked that the family member in question speak on the biography, only that the family member be shown. I suggested A&E could work in some video, but no audio. The producer initially balked at the idea, but in the interest of moving the project forward, eventually agreed. Ironically, when I told Helen how the situation was resolved, she said, "I never wanted that member of my family in the program in the first place." I bit my tongue, but I wanted to respond by saying, "That was what you said in the first place—and you can't have it both ways."

I had Helen and The Ladies over to watch the A&E biography the night it aired, feeling relieved the project had concluded. Helen never liked to watch herself, so she hung out in the next room while the rest of us watched the TV. However, Helen apparently could hear the show.

After the program was over, Helen emerged from the other room on a rant. She was upset with her cousin's interview and felt she "aired our dirty laundry." Neither

I, nor The Ladies, responded, but Helen brought up her cousin's interview on numerous occasions for months. Whatever Helen's cousin said about Helen was so innocuous that I am no longer able to recall what all the fuss was about, though I vividly recall the drama over it.

Helen also had mixed emotions when she was portrayed on a couple of episodes of NBC's *Saturday Night Live*. In one episode, Helen is played by Ana Gasteyer in a less-than-flattering take. The sketch takes place at a press conference with "President" Bill Clinton and "Attorney General" Janet Reno. "Helen" is called on, and she asks a question in an overly shrill, nasally sounding voice. "Janet Reno" responds by saying, "You are a sad old lady!" Helen never appreciated it when anyone mentioned her age.

In another *Saturday Night Live* episode, "Helen" is portrayed by Rachel Dratch, and she is called on by "President" George W. Bush at a news conference, and she says, "Yes, Helen Thomas here, Mr. President. I have served in the press corps since the Kennedy administration, and, yet, do you know you completely ignored me at the last press conference?" Helen had been shunned at real press conferences. As the episode continues, "Helen" attempts another tough question. Chloroform is shoved in her mouth. In a final attempt at asking a question, "Helen" is hit with a poison dart in the neck. The show cuts to "President" Bush standing with the Secret Service. One of the agents smiles while concealing a bamboo shoot in his jacket. The sketch ends with "President" Bush saying "Uh... I couldn't hear the last part of Helen's question. But I do think I know what she wanted to say... and that is, 'Live, from New York, it's Saturday Night!'" The *real* Helen loved it!

We also had several offers to option Helen's memoir, *Front Row at the White House*, along the way. Among those interested was Barbra Streisand. Helen and I met with her in a suite at the Jefferson Hotel on 16th Street in Washington while she was in town. The suite was so hot, it was sweltering, so Helen was a bit shocked when Streisand served piping hot coffee. However, she was even more mystified when she began drinking the coffee from a straw.

Years later, my mom was in town when I got a call from Helen telling me that she "needed" us to meet her at the restaurant in the Capitol Hilton for lunch with "Lassie's mother." My mom figured out we were going to have lunch with actress June Lockhart, and off we went to the meal. My mom was even more shocked than Helen and I were when June drank her coffee through a straw throughout the lunch since Helen and I had witnessed Barbra Streisand doing the same thing previously. As we were departing, Helen whispered to me and my mom, "I think drinking coffee through a straw must be a Hollywood thing."

The HBO
Documentary

After the experience with A&E, I remember not being sure if I was happy or not when HBO approached us about making a documentary on Helen's life. But, then again, it was HBO and its higher-than-average-quality programming. Besides, Helen very much wanted to proceed and was enthusiastic.

The contract negotiations went smoothly, in part because of the professionalism of the HBO people, and also because of their understanding and generosity. Sheila Nevins, the then president of HBO Documentary Films and grand dame of documentaries was, perhaps, even more excited than Helen at the idea of the film, which I thought was a positive.

However, there was trouble almost immediately after the contract was signed. Sheila and others from HBO came to Washington to meet with us and get a sense of what would take place and what they would need from Helen. We met upstairs at the National Press Club in the members' bar. Because we had never met the HBO people in person, Helen and I did not know what they looked like, though I had been speaking with them on the phone for weeks. There were several people sitting at the table with us who were not identified, and they said very little. I assumed they were with HBO. As it turned out, the HBO people assumed they were with us.

Toward the end of the meeting, Sheila said there was a screening that evening of a film they had made on Barry Goldwater, and she asked if Helen and I would like to come. It was at the Georgetown home of *Washington Post* legend Ben Bradlee and his wife, Sally Quinn, a noted journalist in her own right. Helen immediately said we would both be there.

It was at this point the unidentified people spoke up. One of them asked if they could come to the party. Clearly confused, Sheila asked who they were. The man I later came to know as "Richard" explained the documentary was *his* idea. Everyone looked around the table, and Sheila finally told Richard and the woman with him that they were not invited. This is not the last we heard from Richard, including that evening at the screening.

Helen and I arrived at the Georgetown home, and I immediately spotted Richard and his female friend lurking on the sidewalk. I thought it was peculiar since I heard Sheila Nevins specifically tell them not to come, but I was too preoccupied with helping Helen to give it another thought. The party was outside, and there were steep steps leading to the backyard. Helen was in her 80s by this time, so she held onto me as we descended the stairs.

As the evening wore on, there was commotion on the other side of the yard, and I saw Richard and his friend being forcibly escorted up the stairs and presumably out of the house. The following day, the HBO chief counsel and I received phone calls from Richard. He claimed a documentary on Helen's life was his idea, and therefore, he should be a part of the deal and compensated for his efforts.

Richard was becoming a real problem for HBO (and me), so I decided to tell Helen the latest. Much to my horror, Helen told me she had met Richard years before at a party at a restaurant in Los Angeles. She described him as a "hanger-on who doesn't have any money, and a bit of a con-artist"—a fact that became clearer and clearer as the days went by. I wondered to myself why she had never mentioned this previously, but instead I asked Helen if she had ever spoken with Richard about doing a documentary. Helen emphatically assured me she had not. However, in an admitted lapse in poor judgment, Helen said she had run into Richard in the lobby of our building, and not only told him about the HBO documentary, but also told him when and where we were meeting with Sheila and the others with HBO. This explained how the "grifters," as Sheila called them, knew to show up at the Press Club.

Richard became a real problem for everyone involved in the HBO documentary. He turned into a stalker, showing up everywhere. In fact, I was home wrapping presents one evening shortly before Christmas when my doorbell rang. It is highly unusual for anyone to come to my door since I live in a condo building with a front desk that is manned 24/7. Typically, guests are stopped, and a call is made to the homeowner before they are allowed into the elevator.

It was alarming to hear someone at my door, so I froze. After looking out the peephole of my door and seeing a man with a poinsettia plant blocking his face, I crept into another room and called my front desk. I asked if I had a floral delivery, and the man on the desk told me I did not. I asked if anyone had been sent to my door. With the answer being negative, I grew increasingly concerned.

I quietly moved to my door again to see if the man with the poinsettia was still there. He was not only there, but he could hear my movements from the other side of the door. A somewhat familiar sounding voice said, "Flower delivery. Open the door. I can hear you in there." I answered from inside the door, "Please leave the delivery with the front desk in the lobby."

The man was relentless and was growing increasingly belligerent. He banged and pounded on the door and said, "If you don't open the door now, I will break the door down!" I was truly scared. I decided to let the man know that I had identified him and said, "Richard, I know it's you! I don't know what you want, but please just leave!" His reply was unsettling, "I am going to break the door down, and you will be sorry!"

I tiptoed away from the door and phoned the front desk again. Whispering, I frantically told the man answering the phone, "Someone is trying to break my door down!" He said, "Call the police." So I did, explaining I was pretty sure I knew who was on the other side of the door.

The police arrived with sirens blaring. Richard was gone by the time they got to my door, and the police were "convinced" that I had a fight with my boyfriend. As much as I begged to differ, they refused to even take a report.

Shaken, I called my parents and a couple of close friends for advice, including Helen. All of them told me to go to the police station to file a report, and one of my friends offered to accompany me.

Our trip to the police station was fruitless, and I was advised by the police to "hire someone to beat him up." As I left the station, I muttered under my breath, "Yeah, have him beaten up so I get arrested."

I spoke with the attorney at HBO the following day, and he agreed the episode was concerning. I also followed up with Helen. She said she thought Richard had taken the stairwell to and from his new girlfriend's place a few floors below where I lived in our building. Apparently, Richard called Helen to let her know he was living in our building with his girlfriend, who was renting from an owner. Helen hung up on him.

Richard kept up his antics with Helen, select HBO people, and me for what seemed like an eternity. HBO eventually hired a security team to protect everyone involved in the project at official conferences and events. Helen's hospitalization eventually ended Richard's stalking activities with her, but he continued with the rest of us.

However, other than Richard, the HBO project on Helen was exciting. Sheila hired Rory Kennedy to direct the film. Rory is the last child of Robert and Ethel

Kennedy, though Rory never met her father since Ethel was pregnant with her when Bobby was killed on that tragic day in 1968.

Rory was full of energy, talented, and got along well with Helen. When we were looking for a venue to film the one-on-one interviews, Rory suggested we could do them at her mom's house, the renowned Hickory Hill in McLean, Virginia. Helen and I agreed that was good with us if Rory's mother didn't mind the intrusion!

We not only did the interviews at Hickory Hill, but we ate with Mrs. Kennedy, and at each meal she and Helen would reminisce about times past, and their impact on the present. We also learned about Ethel Kennedy's love for bacon.

After a couple of days of eating at Hickory Hill, I observed that bacon was a part of every meal, not just at breakfast. There were bacon bits in salads, filets wrapped in bacon—it was everywhere. I asked Rory if her mom really liked bacon, and she said she did, and to ask her about it. At the next meal, I asked Mrs. Kennedy if she liked bacon. Animated, she told me she *loved* bacon. It was one of her main foods, and she had a "bacon drawer" in their home in Hyannis Port. I had never heard of a bacon drawer, so she explained that it was a drawer to keep bacon warm, at the right temperature and crispness—so you could have bacon any time you wanted. I have never thought of bacon the same way since! Helen joked about wanting a bacon drawer in her home.

Helen's friends, family, and colleagues also agreed to be interviewed for the film, and these took place at

Hickory Hill, too. The documentary was coming along nicely—and then Helen fell ill. Everyone was concerned since Helen was MIA, especially Sheila Nevins. I decided she needed to know what was actually going on, despite Helen's family's wishes that I keep quiet about Helen's hospitalization and induced coma. I trusted that Sheila would not reveal anything to anyone—except to people directly involved in the project, so I gave her a summary of Helen's condition.

This caused sincere concern since it was not known if Helen would make it. Sheila, as well as others associated with the HBO project, called daily, usually more than once a day, for updates. Helen remained in the coma for weeks, her body attempting to heal. Sheila understood that Helen was more than "just a client" to me, so I was particularly touched when a beautiful plant arrived at my door from her.

I was elated when I told Sheila that Helen was out of the coma, and she was expected to survive. But Helen was weak, and she had a long recovery ahead. As the film came together, I was asked to go with HBO to represent Helen at the 2008 Television Critics Association's meeting in Beverly Hills, California.

The meeting showcases upcoming programming before a large group of media focused on TV, and I was honored to be included. We stayed at the luxury hotel, The Peninsula, and we began the trip with a lunch meeting at The Roof Garden restaurant, located near the hotel's rooftop pool and cabanas that offer views of the Los Angeles and Century City skylines. We discussed issues related to showing the documentary, security procedures, and personal apprehensions.

Rory's uncle, Senator Ted Kennedy, had just been diagnosed with brain cancer, and she was worried the press might want details. I had a similar apprehension. Helen's family remained adamant that her illness not be disclosed, so I was concerned the media would ask where Helen had been for weeks, and why she wasn't at the conference. Luckily, both of our fears were needless as nothing came up publicly.

After lunch, we were invited to Sheila's hotel suite to watch the final version of the documentary, *Thank You, Mr. President: Helen Thomas at the White House*. It was an exciting moment in a long process, and I was so sorry that Helen was not there. However, the film was fabulous, and I was flattered to see my name in the credits.

The film was also well received by the TV critics in the eerily lit room at the conference. And we were grateful for HBO's security arrangements since Richard, the stalker, tried to sneak in, but was held back due to the security provisions put in place ahead of time.

Walking around at the reception after our session made it clear Sheila Nevins was a rock star in this setting, and deservedly so. As one of the most noted people in documentary filmmaking, she has been recognized with too-numerous-to-count awards, including Emmys, Peabodys, and Oscars. Most importantly, she is a kind, generous, and empathetic person.

In gearing up for the public release of the film, Rory

handled the interviews since Helen was still in rehab. HBO planned a screening party at the National Press Club, hoping Helen would be well enough to attend. Unfortunately, she didn't make it, but the party was attended by (almost) everyone she knew—and Helen helped with the guest list.

There was a cocktail reception with hors d'oeuvres served at the party. HBO bought copies of Helen's latest book, *The Great White House Breakout*, for the guests, and the crowd cheered when the film was screened.

After the screening, Rory asked me if she and her mom could visit Helen at the rehab center the following morning. I slipped away to call Helen to see if she felt up to it. Helen was ecstatic and told me, "You can't say no to Ethel Kennedy!" She also asked that I be there when they came.

I arrived earlier than the established time of the visit, thinking I would help Helen "primp" a bit for the occasion. Much to my dismay, two women who had befriended Helen at an out-of-town speech were in Helen's room—also awaiting Ethel Kennedy. To this day, I am not sure how these hangers-on, sycophantic women even knew about Helen's illness, but there they were. I was alerted they were in town by Helen earlier since Helen had directed me to "make room" for them at the screening party, even if it meant giving up my place. I don't recall if they came to the party or not and chalked up Helen's bad judgement to her situation. However, Helen had a habit of "picking up" people. I joined her for countless dinners with hairdressers, manicurists, dress shop owners, and other unlikely "friends" impressed by her notoriety and looking to get something out of her.

Helen did not hesitate to bring other people along, unannounced, when she was invited to attend events hosted by these people, either. I remember one occasion when she was invited to attend someone's grandchild's Holy Communion party. She asked me to go with her, as well as one of her nieces. We arrived at the hotel in Bethesda, Maryland, where the party was being held, and much to my horror, it quickly became apparent that the child's grandmother hosting the wedding-like event was not expecting Helen to be accompanied by anyone. Her niece and I stood there aghast as we watched the grandmother direct hotel employees to find a place for us to sit. The rest of the ballroom had round tables beautifully set, each one holding eight people. The hotel employees hauled in a small table for two, prompting the host to tell them to fit two more place settings at one of the round tables. Helen's niece and I awkwardly sat at the tight-fitting table meant for eight, and now accommodating ten people.

There was a video being made as a keepsake for the child. When the videographer arrived at our table, he shoved a microphone in Helen's niece's face, and asked her to say a few kind words. Because neither of us knew the name of the child, Helen's niece said, "Congratulations to..." There was a clumsy pause as she searched for what to call the child. She continued, "to...the kid." We both began snickering, and as we glanced at each other, our laughter became uncontrollable—to the point where we had to excuse ourselves from the embarrassing situation and run to the restroom.

Helen was still wearing a hospital gown when Rory and Ethel Kennedy arrived at the rehab facility, but they greeted each other warmly. The two groupies immediately went into action, physically moving Mrs. Kennedy behind Helen, tossing a camera at me, and demanding I take photos of them posing with the group. Because I didn't know what else to do, I obliged.

When the Kennedys were readying to leave, they asked if I would walk them out to their car. We were barely on the elevator when they both began asking me, "Who are those two women?!?" I simply shrugged my shoulders in exasperation.

Helen's Final Book Tour

Toward the end of Helen's rehab stay, she asked me if I could bring Craig Crawford to see her so they could begin working on their co-authored book. I thought this was a great sign in terms of how Helen was feeling, so the next day Craig and I headed for the rehab facility.

Under the circumstances, at the meeting it was determined that Craig would do the heavy lifting, and he would do the writing with Helen's input. Craig is a brilliant writer who had his own books published previously. He also is far more organized than Helen could have ever hoped to be, so I thought this was a good plan. In reality, Craig ended up simply writing the whole book with very little input from Helen, but Craig made a concerted effort to write from Helen's point of view. And he did so effectively, even when his opinion differed from that of Helen's on some issues.

Listen Up, Mr. President was published in 2009, and then, as every author knows, the real work began—promoting the book. By this time, Helen's health had improved enough that she was back to work, covering the White House, and writing her opinion column for Hearst (she resigned from UPI after it was purchased by Sun Myung Moon, the leader of the Unification Church, or Moonies, in 2000, and eventually accepted a job with Hearst). Helen was insistent that she wanted to promote the book, but she had a necessary team of full-time nurse's aides at home to assist her with dressing and changing her colostomy bag.

We collectively decided we would have one of the nurse's aides travel with us, and I was glad when Helen chose Abie, a wonderful woman who came to America from Sierra Leone.

One of our first trips was to Orlando, Craig's hometown. Craig stayed with his parents, Bill and Toby. Helen, Abie, and I stayed at a club Craig's parents belonged to that was about five minutes from their home.

The club, Bay Hill, is an Arnold Palmer property, and was known as the winter home of the golf legend. The nicely appointed rooms opened up to a private patio overlooking the golf course. One morning before our day of book activities began, I was sitting on the patio in the soft bathrobe provided in my room, and an early morning golfer's ball landed next to my foot. He was extremely apologetic and even asked if he could collect his ball from the patio. I wondered how the penalty shot would work!

Helen and Craig signed books and did interviews in Orlando and the surrounding area, including Daytona. We ate meals with Craig's parents, and it was a successful trip.

When we returned from Orlando, Helen and Craig crisscrossed the country for book signings and media, sometimes individually and sometimes together. Abie and I accompanied Helen on all of her trips. They did a lot in Washington as well.

However, it was the last joint trip that, upon reflection, was a foreshadowing of what would eventually come to pass. Helen and Craig were scheduled for media and book signings in New York City. We debated how we would get to New York from DC—by train, plane, or car. Helen became insistent of her desire to go by car, so Craig said he would drive.

We set out for the Big Apple in the morning with Craig at the wheel, Helen and Abie in the back seat, and me helping navigate from the front passenger seat. We stopped once for a snack and gas, and after our stop, Helen fell asleep.

Helen awoke from her nap on a rant. Out of the blue, she shouted, "The Holocaust Memorial should have never been in Washington!" Craig and I exchanged glances, and Abie sat silently next to Helen. Nobody uttered a word. So, Helen repeated her words, carrying on like her life depended on it. The silence emanating from the others in the car was deafening. Craig finally spoke up, "Where should they have built the Holocaust Memorial?" Helen replied in an angry tone, "Germany, of course!" Nobody said anything further until we arrived in New York.

However, I knew Helen well enough to know that this was not the end of it. When she got on any topic related to Israel, Arab countries, or anything remotely connected to the Middle East, it was as though a switch turned on in Helen, and she became a different person. This was true no matter the setting: at the White House, presidential press conferences, speeches when asked a question on a related topic, or a simple social gathering with friends.

In fact, there had been several previous incidents that I sadly witnessed. The first one involved a dinner at Ayesha's with a friend from high school and her fiancé, a Jewish man. I don't recall the specific topic, but the conversation turned to something regarding the Middle East. The give and take became heated as Helen hurled insults at the only Jewish person at the table. He held his own, but in the end, the couple completely stopped talking to me over my association with Helen. Subsequently, when I tried to talk to Helen about the loss of good friends, she brushed me off, proclaiming, "That's why you should never marry a Jew."

On another occasion, Helen and I were having dinner at an upscale Chinese restaurant, Mr. K's, with two Jewish academics who had befriended Helen. Because it was Chinese food, I guess Helen assumed we would share some dishes. She proceeded to order pork dumplings, hot and sour soup (which has pork in it), a pork entree, a shrimp dish, and pork lo mein. Because our guests kept kosher, one of them gently told Helen that neither of them would be able to eat any of the food. Helen responded by saying, "Don't give me that crap with those old, barbaric rules. They were created for food safety long ago." I mustered up the courage to say that I would also like a beef, chicken, or vegetable entree. Helen shot me a look to try to shut me up, but I ordered the dishes anyway. A number of years later, the same women walked out of a dinner at Ayesha's due to Helen's attacks on Jews. We never saw them again.

Without a doubt, the most horrifying episode, up until that point, occurred just days after the September 11 terrorist attacks on our country. I was having dinner at Ayesha's with a friend who had grown up in New York City. His father and two brothers still lived there. My friend was visibly shaken over the loss of dozens of people he and his family knew who were killed as a result of the terrorists in New York. Helen walked into the restaurant and sat down with us. After ordering a bottle of red wine, she asked what we were discussing. When I explained, Helen got out of her seat, jumping up and down, periodically slapping the table, and all the while screaming at my friend, "You Jew! You Jew!" She then picked up her bottle of wine and strutted to a table in the other room. We could see Helen at her new table, and my friend kept asking me if he should apologize to Helen and ask her to rejoin us. I told him that he had nothing to apologize for, and Helen owed him an apology.

So, in light of all these incidents, I was worried about the first book event later that evening in New York after Helen's outburst in the car. The format for the program was to have Craig "interview" Helen, as they had done many times over again. I was confident nothing Craig asked would set Helen off. But I needed to somehow get control over the audience Q&A that followed the program for fear someone would ask a question about the Middle East.

I talked with Craig (without our traveling companions) after we checked in at the Cornell Club where we were staying (there was an event there the following day). After discussing Helen's outburst in the car and how awkward it felt for both of us, Craig and I decided that I would ask the hosting organization to have people submit their questions in writing to me.

Helen was still on her rant on the way to the event that evening, though the sights and sounds of the city eventually refocused the conversation in the cab we took to get to the venue. By the time we arrived, Helen had calmed down substantially.

As expected, the program portion of the event with Craig "interviewing" Helen went well. While the program was taking place, people submitted written questions that someone collected and brought to me where I was sitting in a chair off to the side. I was so glad we had decided on written questions. There were more than a few audience members who asked something that I knew would lead Helen to say something publicly that would only lead to trouble. When I saw these questions, I made sure nobody was looking at me, and I quietly slipped those index cards into my purse. When I handed Craig the stack of questions for Helen, I was confident there was no danger of Helen saying anything inappropriate.

That is, until the private dinner afterward. There were some people of Lebanese background at the dinner who got Helen all riled up again, so Craig and I talked with Helen's publisher who had come to the event, hoping she wouldn't overhear Helen's comments that could be construed by some as anti-Semitic, though I knew Helen was certainly entitled to express her views.

Meantime, Craig, Abie, and I noticed that Helen had barely eaten all day. On the way up to New York, Helen only had a cup of coffee, and she only pushed the food around at the private dinner, despite the waitstaff piling it on her plate.

The next morning, Craig, Abie, and I met for breakfast at the Cornell Club, and Helen only ordered coffee. We had lunch at the celebrated Algonquin Hotel's Round Table restaurant, noted for its literary history with Dorothy Parker and other writers. Helen ordered soup and ate only a couple of teaspoons. We all were becoming increasingly worried, and the situation reminded me of my trip with Helen to Delaware before she nearly died.

By the time we left New York, Helen essentially had only "eaten" coffee and a few bites of actual food. On the drive back to Washington, we stopped for lunch at the usual rest stop, which offered fast food delicacies found off the turnpike. Abie and Craig made it my "job" to see if I could get Helen to eat something. I got Helen situated at a table and asked her what sounded good. She said she only wanted coffee. Frustrated, but taking my "assignment" to heart, I finally got Helen to agree to some ice cream.

However, when I returned to the table with the ice cream, Helen was less than enthusiastic, occasionally pushing the plastic spoon around in the small bowl.

Because the others were still waiting for their food, I took the opportunity while we were alone to ask Helen if she was feeling okay. As I anticipated, she bit my head off, shouting at me, "Why does it matter to you if I eat? Go get yourself some food and leave me the hell alone!" All of this felt eerily familiar to the previous time Helen wouldn't eat, and I grew increasingly worried.

I slunk away from the table, leaving Helen with her melting ice cream, and went to find Craig and Abie. When I saw them, I asked if they would meet me outside the entry door, to discuss Helen's condition.

We stood outside the door of the rest area debating what, if anything, we could or should do. It was decided I would call one of Helen's nieces who lives in the Washington area and explain what was happening to see if she could help. Hesitantly, Helen's niece agreed to call her aunt on her cell in half an hour when we would be back in the car.

We got Helen situated in the car and nervously waited for the call. When it came, there was no missing Helen's reaction. She screamed at her niece just as she had yelled at me inside the food court at the rest stop. However, when Helen got off the phone, she said nothing—and nobody else uttered a word, either.

The trip to New York weighed heavily on my mind when we got back to Washington, but I was hopeful Helen's nieces would get her to see a doctor. Hopefully, with some medical attention, Helen would be back to her old self. Little did I know what all of this would lead to.

No Turning Back

It was a warm Friday on June 4, 2010, and I was inside with the air conditioning running strongly. My tech guy was sitting at the desk in my office installing a new computer, so I planted myself on a couch in another room within shouting distance of my office. I had a small notebook computer at my side, and I was returning what seemed like an endless list of phone messages.

My tech guy periodically shouted from my office, "You're getting a lot of emails!" I didn't really think anything of it since my inbox is constantly full. I couldn't check my email because it wasn't working on the notebook laptop I had with me—an issue that was probably related to whatever the tech guy was doing.

I had not spoken to Helen yet, but I knew I would since we usually talked several times a day about speaking events and media, dinner plans, or the political issues du jour. I did, however, receive a phone call regarding Helen that was disturbing, to say the least.

Helen's boss at Hearst called me, something which was not unusual, so I initially didn't think anything of it. However, when he said he had his boss on the phone with him, I knew something was up. He didn't beat around the bush, either. He said, "We are about to fire Helen, but we believe she deserves representation. How quickly can you get over to our offices?"

After what Helen's boss said registered with me, I responded, "I beg your pardon?" To which he replied, "So, you don't know?" I said, "Know what?" I couldn't imagine what Helen had done that would put her job in jeopardy. The boss said, "We can play you the audio, but you really need to see the video that's gone viral." I braced myself as the audio came over the phone. It was between Helen and a rabbi—I later learned it was Rabbi David Nesenoff. The audio from the one-minute video posted on RabbiLive.com went like this:

QUESTION: *Any comments on Israel? We're asking everyone today.*
HELEN: *Tell them to get the hell out of Palestine.*
QUESTION: *Any better comments?*
HELEN: *Remember. These people are occupied. And it's their land. It's not German, and it's not Poland's.*
QUESTION: *So where should they go? What should they do?*
HELEN: *Go home.*
QUESTION: *Where's home?*
HELEN: *Poland. Germany.*
QUESTION: *So, the Jews should go back to Poland and Germany?*
HELEN: *And America, and everywhere else.*

Apparently, Helen was coming out of the White House after a reception hosted by President Barack

Obama and First Lady Michelle Obama celebrating Jewish Heritage Month on May 27 that Rabbi Nesenoff, his teenage son, and his son's friend attended. The trio spotted Helen on her way out and called her over, initially asking Helen if she had any advice for the boys who wanted to be journalists. Helen was always good about stopping to chat with people who recognized her. There was no mistaking they were Jewish. All three were wearing the Jewish skullcaps known as yarmulkes.

About a week later, Rabbi Nesenoff posted the exchange captured on video on his website. That was June 3. I knew nothing of the encounter until the following day when I received the phone call from Helen's bosses at Hearst.

I was speechless when I heard the audio over the phone and dumbfounded that Helen could make such inappropriate, hateful remarks. I was hopeful her words were taken out of context, even though Helen had become increasingly vocal about how she viewed Israel in recent months. Helen's own words when she left UPI and began writing an opinion column for Hearst were running through my mind like a tape on a loop: "I censored myself for 50 years when I was a reporter. Now I wake up every morning and ask myself, 'Who do I hate today?'"

I quickly gathered my thoughts and asked the Hearst men if I could have a little time to speak with Helen privately before they took any action. They responded by telling me that if I didn't get back to them quickly, they would have no choice but to proceed to fire her.

I hung up the phone and immediately called Helen.

When she picked up, her voice sounded nasally, so I knew she had been crying and was aware of the situation. Time was of the essence, so I thought I may as well be upfront with her. I said, "I guess you know you are in big trouble. I just hung up with your bosses, and they are about to fire you. Tell me what happened. Why did you make those awful comments?" Helen began to cry faucets of tears.

When Helen finally calmed down, I told her that I thought there were a number of options that might save her job. She never answered the "why she made the comments" question I had asked her, but I assumed her crying meant she was sorry. I suggested she post an apology on her website, which my company maintained on her behalf. I also suggested I try to get her on a show such as *Larry King Live* to apologize and explain what she meant. *Larry King Live* was a talk show that aired on CNN at the time.

My suggestions did not go over well with Helen. She began screaming at me in a way I had never heard before. She said she meant every word of what she had said, and she did not intend to apologize, nor did she feel she owed anyone an apology. I was horrified, but decided I had to put on my agent hat to get her to do the right thing. I tried reasoning with her. I eventually was able to get Helen to agree to let us post a statement on her website.

While Helen worked on the statement, I called her boss at Hearst. I asked him if he thought an apologetic statement on the website would be enough to save her job. He said he didn't know, but he would take it into account. By the end of the conversation, he agreed he would not make a decision until the following week, but he was emphatic that Helen "lay low" over the weekend and to try not to say anything publicly about her remarks.

We posted Helen's statement on her website—which I did not think went far enough to apologize, but it was her choice. It said, "I deeply regret my comments I made last week regarding the Israelis and the Palestinians. They do not reflect my heartfelt belief that peace will come to the Middle East only when all parties recognize the need for mutual respect and tolerance. May that day come soon."

Meanwhile, my tech guy told me I was getting so many emails that they were crashing the server, so I finally took a look at them. There were thousands of emails, and they were still pouring in. No wonder the tech man said I was getting a lot of emails! They were a mixed bag, but the vast majority were unkind at best and threatening at worst.

The phone began ringing, too. All of the lines lit up at once, and it did not stop. The voice messages were significantly similar to the emails that continued to land in my inbox. It seems a lot of people blamed me for Helen's comments to Rabbi Nesenoff. Or, some could not believe I could "represent such a mean, horrible, anti-Semite." But some of the emails and messages were downright frightening. I remember one voicemail that said, "You deserve to die, and I will see to it that you do." There were other death threats, too, some more overt than others.

I called Helen to let her know the statement was up on her website and tell her about my last conversation with her boss. She blew up at me again, "I will not lay low, and you do not own me." I explained I was only repeating what her boss had asked me to pass along. She said, "Don't give me that crap," and slammed the phone down. I repeatedly tried calling her back, but each time, Helen hung up on me.

The hateful messages and emails continued. I was in tears. Friends who had heard about Helen's remarks stopped by to see how I was handling everything, since they couldn't get through to me on the phone—though they had no idea what my day had been like.

My friends and I talked, and talked, and talked. I explained how I felt conflicted. On the one hand, hateful speech has no place in the world, let alone in our country. On the other hand, Helen was my friend, so I felt her pain. Deep down, I suspected Helen was humiliated, but she was covering it up with anger. How does one reconcile caring so deeply about someone who made such hateful remarks? Years later, I related to the *Today Show*'s co-anchor Savannah Guthrie's shock and horror over her friend and colleague, Matt Lauer's, sudden resignation from NBC when she expressed similar emotions over the accusations of Lauer's horrific behavior toward women.

I was exhausted by the ringing phone and continuous emails by the time Sunday rolled around. The death threats kept coming, and some now included threatening my other clients. I was reaching a better understanding of why there was no peace in the Middle

East. I had not heard from Helen, despite my repeated attempts to reach out, including knocking on the door of her home. It was clear Helen had no intention of talking to me, let alone taking my advice.

In light of this, as well as the fact that I disagreed with Helen's remarks, I decided the right thing to do was to resign as her agent. It was one of the most difficult decisions I have ever made. I ultimately paid a high price for my decision, but I still believe it was the right one. As Helen often told me herself, "Do the right thing, and you will have no regrets."

I tried one last time to call Helen, waited an hour, and then wrote her a letter, which I left taped to her front door. Here is most of it:

June 6, 2010
Helen Thomas
(address redacted)

Dear Helen,
I write to you with a heavy heart, and I love you beyond words.

Unfortunately, I am not going to be able to work with you as your agent anymore. I have received over 14,000 emails (as of now), as well as hundreds of phone calls, threatening me—and threatening to ruin my business (and to ruin all of my other clients) if I continue to represent you. I have printed a sample of the emails if you would like to see them.

This is by far the most difficult decision I have ever had to make, and I do so as I cry on my computer keyboard. Unfortunately, the world is a crazy place, and I am not equipped to weather the storm. I wish I could fight the good fight with you.

I am so sorry, and I want you to know that I will always admire you both as a person, and as a journalist who has had such an illustrious career—a career that has broken so many barriers to make the world a better place for my generation and all that follow. I truly wish you had not spoken those words.

I am hopeful that we will be able to maintain our incredible friendship. It is more meaningful to me than you will ever know. After my parents, you have been the most important person in my life, and I love you dearly.

Please know that I am still here for you if I can help in any way.

If you think you can, please call me. I would like to see if we can get together tomorrow.

With heartfelt love,
Diane

I sobbed when I got back to my place. The phone rang (yet again), and this time I was hopeful it would be Helen, so I glanced at the caller ID. It was Craig Crawford, so I picked up the phone.

Craig was noticeably upset. Apparently, he was having a similar experience with the emails and calls because he had co-authored *Listen Up, Mr. President* with Helen. Craig was very much in the public eye, having resigned a few months earlier as a frequent political commentator for NBC/MSNBC, and he was now the publisher of Trail Mix, a political news commenting forum.

It upset me that Craig was also being put through the ringer. I felt responsible since I had suggested he and Helen co-author the book. And I considered Craig a friend.

We decided I would give Craig a statement about my resignation to post on Trail Mix, and Craig would simply agree with the statement. I spent some time writing what I hoped was something that expressed my distaste for Helen's inappropriate, inflammatory remarks—that were by now making worldwide news—yet conveyed a sense of Helen's accomplishments. This is what was posted:

For Immediate Release
Contact: Diane Nine
202-XXX-XXXX
June 6, 2010

It is with a heavy heart that Nine Speakers, Inc. announces its resignation as the agent for Helen Thomas, Dean of the White House Press Corps.

Ms. Thomas has had an esteemed career as a journalist, and she has been a trailblazer for women, helping others in her profession and beyond.

However, in light of recent events, Nine Speakers is no longer able to represent Ms. Thomas, nor can we condone her comments on the Middle East.

Nine Speakers will continue to enthusiastically represent all of our other current and future clients.

When Craig posted it, he wrote beneath it: "I agree

with my agent's statement, and I will no longer be working with Helen on our book projects."

Putting out the statement resulted in a flurry of phone calls from media, but after talking to POLITICO, I decided to avoid these calls, at least for the time being.

I did, however, answer a call from Helen's boss at Hearst.

Helen's Resignation

When I saw Helen's boss on the caller ID, I picked up the phone. An animated voice on the other end told me he was on his way to Helen's home to fire her, and he asked me to meet him there. I explained that I had just resigned as Helen's agent, so I didn't think it would be appropriate for me to be there. However, I suggested I could try to get one of Helen's family members who lived in the area to be there. I hoped I could reach one of them. Despite everything, I didn't want Helen to be alone when the axe fell.

I was luckily able to reach one of Helen's relatives. When I explained why I would not be able to be with Helen, her family member immediately hung up on me. At least, I assumed, someone would be there with Helen.

Helen's soon-to-be-former boss called me after he left Helen's home. He said he found Helen's family to be of no help, and there was a lot of crying. However, he said he agreed to allow Helen to resign rather than be fired. Helen's resignation would be announced on Monday. My heart was breaking since I knew how much Helen's job meant to her. She often said, "I think I'll work all my life and never retire. When you're having fun, why stop having fun?"

The announcement of Helen's resignation did little to calm the waters, and the aftermath was not fun. I was left to respond to organizations wanting to cancel speeches and awards. There was a whole schedule that had to be addressed, and Helen was still not speaking to me. In the end, Helen was persona non grata. Every single organization on the lengthy schedule cancelled. I thought about the irony of how long it had taken to put the calendar together, and how quickly it unraveled.

Helen's colleagues with the White House Correspondents' Association issued a harsh statement calling her remarks to the rabbi "indefensible." Her alma mater, Wayne State University, retired the Spirit of Diversity in Media award in her name. The Society of Professional Journalists retired their award in Helen's name. Even President Obama was critical. In a television interview on NBC, he said, "Her comments were offensive. It's a shame, because Helen is someone who has been a correspondent through I don't know how many presidents. She was a real institution in Washington. But I think she made the right decision (to retire)."

It seemed as though everyone had to weigh in. President George W. Bush's press secretary, Ari Fleischer, called Helen's remarks "appalling." President Obama's press secretary, Robert Gibbs, called the comments "offensive and reprehensible."

However, Helen did have some supporters. Arab

organizations cried foul. A handful of politicians and media threw their support behind Helen. Even some of Helen's colleagues at the White House came out in her support. Of course, Helen's family and some friends, including The Ladies, continued to have Helen's back. Some of The Ladies were kind to me as well.

I was initially glad that there were some people who could be a comfort to Helen. After all, she had never really been without a job her entire life, and the White House and her job had always been her life. Helen was now 89 years old and not in the best of health. So, I was privately relieved that she had people around her.

I didn't initially know just how poor Helen's health actually was until one of The Ladies told me she had learned that Helen was almost in kidney failure and had begun dialysis. In discussing all of this with a friend who is a medical doctor—and Jewish—she told me that while she was not excusing Helen's behavior, especially as a Jewish woman, poor kidney function can lead to cognitive disorders, including something resembling dementia. She speculated that this may be what occurred with Helen. My mind immediately went back to our trip to New York with Craig Crawford, and the combination of Helen not wanting to eat and her non sequitur about where the Holocaust Memorial should have been located.

Meanwhile, Helen could not allow herself the luxury of retiring and fading happily into the sunset. Instead, she was seen and heard in various media interviews, and she delivered a couple of speeches to Arab organizations. In some people's minds, she was only making matters worse. However, she was hired by the owner of a small, weekly newspaper, *The Falls Church (VA) News-Press*, as a contributing columnist. And Helen would not be silenced.

In an interview with a small radio station in Marion, Ohio, Helen told the host that she only apologized for her comments to the rabbi because people were upset, but she "has the same feelings about Israel's aggression and brutality." On CNN's *Joy Behar Show*, Helen was combative and defensive. She said of the Jews in Israel, "Why do they have to go anywhere? They aren't being persecuted. They don't have the right to take other people's land." In the same interview, Helen was asked if she was an anti-Semite, and she responded with, "Hell no. I'm a Semite. Of Arab background. They're (Jews), not Semites."

At a speech to an Arab organization in Dearborn, Michigan, Helen told reporters, "I paid a price, but it's worth it to speak the truth." And, in the speech itself, she ranted, "Congress, the White House, Hollywood, and Wall Street are owned by Zionists."

Helen even did an interview with *Playboy* magazine that was in the April 2011 edition that raised a few eyebrows when she dug her heels in again.

And, I got continuous interview requests from around the world, though I only chose to do two additional interviews subsequent to the one with POLITICO the day I resigned as Helen's agent. These interviews were with a journalist-client and with a high school friend who hosted a local radio show in the Detroit area. I only did the interviews because I knew and trusted the journalists, but I did not believe there was anything to be gained for me—or Helen—by continuing to stoke the fires. Besides, my heart was still broken over both Helen's remarks to the rabbi and my subsequent "breakup" with someone who had been so important to me. I was holding out hope there would be a way to repair my relationship with Helen. While I could never bring myself to support or understand Helen's words, I couldn't keep myself from loving her.

However, circumstances led me to believe there was no chance of getting Helen to even speak to me again. Helen's family had totally turned against me, and some of the "users" whom Helen previously asked me to help keep at bay swooped in to "help" Helen. These people, along with a couple of Helen's semi-retired journalist friends, set out to make my life miserable.

One of the journalist friends wrote an article for an online media watchdog organization that really sent me over the edge. I think my response to her below is self-explanatory as to the accusations made:

"As a reporter, I would have thought you might have at least tried to get your facts right, especially since you are writing for such a prestigious media watchdog group and are considered one of the most admired reporters in the country. I always thought real journalists would, at the very least, call the subject of a story for a comment. You did not even attempt to contact me, and you certainly are not factually correct when you claim that I "bit the hand that feeds me." Perhaps your view of this is understandably colored by your friendship with Helen.

My business as an author's agent and as a speaker's bureau did not profit significantly from Helen's contracts. Many of the speaking engagements which were set up by my company were either pro bono events for which Helen requested we donate our time, or they were often so low paying that we did not even take a fee in order to make it work for Helen. I have contracts that go back years to prove this point. Frankly, I never overtly objected to any of this, as I considered Helen to be one of my friends, and our family ties go back to my grandmother.

On other matters, I actually wrote sections (chapters) of several of Helen's books since she was late in meeting her contractual publishing deadlines. I did so without payment or even credit. I doubt many other people would have done this without being paid. Further, I arranged for Helen to make a LOT of money off of several of my other clients for doing little or nothing. In fact, Helen did not do any significant work on her last TWO books. She simply collected the LARGE advances, and any subsequent royalties as they came along. Again, none of us objected to this arrangement because of our affection for Helen.

In connection with both speeches and book promotions, and because Helen needed me, I often traveled with Helen at my own expense—especially in recent years when Helen wasn't as physically capable as she used to be. Though this gesture frequently cut into my paying work, I felt a sincere obligation to help take care of this woman whom I have admired since I was a child.

In addition, in my opinion, Helen often used poor judgment in surrounding herself with OTHER people who were after her fame and money. Several of these crooked individuals impacted me personally and professionally—and my father, who is a well-respected attorney, represented me AND Helen for FREE—over matters that should have never taken place.

In fact, my entire family has been nothing but kind and generous to Helen. Each year my mother lovingly (at her own expense and time) did the invitations for Helen's annual Christmas party (including postage and a pre-stamped RSVP card)—as well as paying for party favors for 100+ people. I was the one who personally donated my time for the "grunt" work for this occasion to pull it all together. We did these things because we loved Helen, not because we thought we were taking advantage of her.

When I stopped counting, I had received approximately 40,000 email messages regarding this matter (Helen's comments to the rabbi). The vast majority of these were not in support of what Helen said to the blogger (rabbi) who taped her response for the world to hear. However, MANY of the messages have come to me with overt death threats if I continued to represent Ms. Thomas, and other clients who had relationships with Helen were point-blank told to publicly disavow their relationship with her. I find it interesting that you think I should support Helen in spite of what she has said publicly, though I wonder why everyone from Hearst to the President of the United States has not defended her statements? Am I to assume by your comments to me that you support Helen's comments?

In summation, Helen made out generously as a result of being represented by my firm, and I did NOT make "a lot of money" off of Helen. In fact, over time, I was most likely in a deficit position if you add up the amount of free work I have done for Helen. And, Helen has certainly never once asked to unwind our agency agreement or to have someone *else represent her. She had it too good. . .and I loved her too much.*

To Helen's undying credit, she has always told me to "do the right thing, and you will never regret it." I did the right thing. Hate speech is not acceptable.

I am asking for a formal retraction of your inaccurate and potentially libelous statement....

Thank you,
Diane S. Nine"

There were other unflattering articles as well, but at some point, I simply gave up. The death threats continued, and some friends in law enforcement advised me of some measures I could take to try to keep myself safe, which I implemented. I also gave up the notion of having any kind of a relationship with Helen.

I lived in fear of what would happen if I inadvertently ran into Helen or individuals in her new circle of friends. I stopped eating at Mama Ayesha's, but we lived in the same condo building. Several times, I arrived home after an evening out and noticed Helen being dropped off at the building's front door. Friends and I would drive past the building, around the neighborhood—until we thought enough time had passed to be sure I wouldn't bump into Helen when I entered my building to go up the elevator to my home.

The combination of all of this made me feel immense stress, and that led to not eating or sleeping well. My friends, family, and even some clients tried to help, but I just couldn't shake the feeling that my world was crumbling. From losing my longest close friend in

Helen, to my lasting astonishment at Helen's remarks to the rabbi, to continuous media requests, to repeated death threats, to everyone I saw and spoke with asking if there were any updates on the situation, I needed a break.

I got a break. But not the kind I anticipated.

Different Strokes

About a year had passed since Helen made her hateful remarks to the rabbi, and while there had been some diminishing of all the drama, a lot of the turmoil still existed. I hadn't been feeling well, not just emotionally, but physically. At times, I felt as though I couldn't catch my breath, and I had an overall feeling I was not well. But I couldn't pinpoint exactly what hurt or what was wrong with me. I felt tired, but I chalked it up to not getting enough sleep. In the past, I would have told Helen about all of this, but that was no longer an option.

I had dinner one evening at a friend's place, and while I was there, my calves began to cramp. I eventually fell asleep on the couch, and when I woke up, I barely had enough energy to get home.

I woke up feeling worse the following morning, so I decided not to work, something that was highly unusual for me. Another friend called to ask if she could stop by. I told her I wasn't feeling well and was still wearing my nightshirt, but to come over. This ended up being a potentially life-saving visit.

Not far into my friend's arrival, the phone rang. When I tried to stand to answer it, the cramping in my calves was so severe that I could barely get up, so I asked my friend to answer it. The caller was a doctor friend from college. I had spoken to her a couple of days previously and told her I wasn't feeling well, so she wanted to know how I was doing. While my two friends were chatting, I began to feel odd.

The friend with me described my actions to the doctor on the phone, and she kept asking me what was happening. I remember grabbing my arm, which felt numb. Then my arm felt okay, but my leg went numb.

I thought, "What's happening to me? I can't move my right leg. I feel strange. I can't seem to answer my friend sitting across from me. She keeps asking me if I'm okay. What is happening?!? Why can't I talk?"

Luckily, the doctor recognized my friend's description of my actions and told my friend to hang up, call 911, and tell them she was with someone who might be having a stroke.

Then there were sirens in the distance, and they were getting closer. My friend was running around gathering up my purse and a change of clothes. There was a heavy knock on the door. Paramedics came into the room where I sat on a couch. They took my vitals and asked me questions. I understood what they were asking, but I didn't seem to be able to get the words out to answer them. I replied by nodding and using other body language.

The paramedics put me on a gurney and strapped me down. They wheeled me down the hall of my condo building. It was crowded on the elevator with the gurney, the paramedics, and my friend. They moved quickly through the lobby of the building. I noticed people staring at me in the lobby.

We were situated in an ambulance, and I heard the paramedics on a speaker phone. My friend was in the front of the ambulance. She was speaking to me in a loud, but calming, voice. I found this reassuring. The doctors were giving the paramedics directions over the speakerphone.

One of the paramedics told me that we were on our way to George Washington University Hospital. I still couldn't talk, so I nodded my head to let him know I understood. The same paramedic kept telling me repeatedly, "You may be having a stroke. You may be having a stroke!"

I thought, "This can't be real. How can I be having a stroke? I'm not old enough to have a stroke. I'm only 49 years old."

When the ambulance arrived at the hospital, I was rushed to the back of the emergency room. I was surrounded by all kinds of medical professionals who poked and prodded me. The next thing I knew, I was being wheeled into an MRI. It was much more claustrophobic than I remembered from years ago when I had an ankle injury.

They determined that I not only suffered one stroke, but actually two back-to-back strokes. It seemed like hours passed before I was finally taken to a room on the fourth floor of George Washington University Hospital—the stroke unit floor. I was hooked up to all kinds of monitors and medical equipment.

Apparently, my friend let a slew of people know what

was happening, and other friends arrived. Someone told me that my parents had been called and would be arriving from Michigan in the morning.

Some friends ended up spending the night at the hospital to stay with me. I will be forever grateful to them.

When my parents arrived the following morning, and I saw their faces when they walked into my room, I thought I was going to have another stroke. They looked sick with worry, but they were trying to be positive for my sake.

My leg was still paralyzed, but I was beginning to be able to speak—just words, and some phrases. The doctors said I had "expressive aphasia"—when a person understands everything and can follow directions but can't verbally express themselves.

I didn't know what the future might hold, nor did I know what had caused my strokes. That is, until later.

I was still in ICU a couple of days after my stroke when Helen's nurse's aide, Abie, showed up in my room. Apparently, when one is taken out through a building's lobby on a gurney, it becomes building gossip. Abie said Helen was so concerned that she cried when she heard about me, and Abie had brought me a plush, stuffed monkey from Helen—who knew I had collected monkeys since I was a child. Abie talked about Helen and how she was doing without her job covering the White House.

When Abie left, a doctor came into my room and said, "I couldn't help overhearing your conversation with your guest. Are you THAT agent?" Because I could barely talk, I nodded my head affirmatively. The doctor then said, "No wonder you had a stroke! Stress can add to underlying medical issues."

Days seemed like weeks, and weeks seemed like months while I recovered, but friends and family visited and called regularly to keep me encouraged. I thought things were looking up in terms of repairing my relationship with Helen when I had a surprise visit from one of Helen's nieces, her husband, and their daughter. This was the first time I had seen anyone from Helen's family subsequent to her resignation from Hearst. There was a lot of crying and hugging, and it felt good.

Three and a half weeks after my medical emergency, I was sprung from the hospital using a cane to walk, and—though it was still difficult—speaking clearly. Learning to walk and talk again were the hardest hurdles I ever overcame, and in the end, I am grateful I made a complete recovery.

A friend picked me up to take me home. I was elated to be back in my own place with my cat, who poured affection on me, making it clear she had missed her human. The following evening, my first visitor was Helen's great-niece, the one who had visited me while I was in the hospital. I was so glad that Helen's family seemed to be coming around and willing to bury the hatchet.

However, I would have never guessed that my second visitor would be Helen. A friend offered to cook dinner for us. I have to admit feeling a little anxious, but I really needed her friendship again. The evening seemed like old times, and Helen insisted she wanted to take the group to dinner at Ayesha's later that week. Life was good again.

Helen and I never discussed the reasons behind our temporary breakup, including her remarks to the rabbi. I guess some things are best left unsaid. At that moment in time, after all I had been through, I just needed to feel a sense of normalcy without delving into the whys of it all.

Some members of Helen's family continued to give me the cold shoulder, as did Helen's increasing number of sycophantic "friends" who had made themselves available to her while we were not speaking to one another. But I tried not to let these people bother me. Helen and I knew in our hearts that we mattered to each other.

My health gradually improved, and at times, even surpassed my doctors' expectations. I was walking without a cane after just a week of outpatient physical therapy, and at the end of the second week, my PT suggested I just needed to practice walking, and to consider getting a trainer. I went to one session of outpatient speech therapy where I was given a verbal test. I guess I passed with flying colors since I was told I didn't need any more speech therapy, and I should just practice talking.

Dinnertime and Death

Among Helen's family members who had not exactly warmed to the idea of Helen embracing me again were some who live in the Washington area. I don't know if Helen told them we were back to periodically having dinner again, but I figured it didn't matter. Helen lived almost two years after I had my stroke, and we enjoyed our dinners together.

On one occasion, it had been more than a week since I had last seen Helen, though I knew her health was declining dramatically, she looked even frailer than usual on our last visit at her home. I also knew that Helen had hospice care at her home.

On July 19, 2013, I was working in my office when the phone rang in the late afternoon. It was Helen's niece who said, "If you want to see Aunt Helen, I think you need to come now. She has been asking for you."

I dropped what I was doing and immediately went to Helen's. She was lying on a hospital bed in her living room, just steps away from the small entryway. I acknowledged the few people sitting in the room, and I looked at Helen on the bed. Her eyes opened as I leaned in to hear her trying to speak. In a barely audible whisper, Helen said, "I'm sorry."

Not knowing what to make of this, I looked around the room. The others were chatting quietly. I leaned back over the bed at Helen, whose eyes were already closed again, and simply said, "I love you." Helen did not open her eyes.

I took a seat with the others. We talked a bit, but mostly we just sat in silence on our death watch. After a couple of hours, it was clear that Helen wasn't going to rebound, so I decided to go back to my place. I hugged Helen's nieces and gave Helen's hand a squeeze, choking back my tears.

As soon as I was out the door, my tears flowed for the inevitable loss of my friend. I thought I would need a mop to sop up all the tears. I cried a lot that evening while contemplating what Helen's last words to me meant. Did "I'm sorry" mean she was apologizing for her behavior surrounding her comments to the rabbi, or was she "sorry" she would never see me again? I chose to believe it was a little of both.

The next morning, I learned that Helen passed away in the wee hours of the morning on July 20. She was 92 years old, and just weeks away from her 93rd birthday.

There was considerable media coverage of Helen's death, and while her career-ending incident was mentioned, it was not the focus of most of the news reports. Instead, they spoke of Helen's many years of reporting on the White House, more than any other individual. They talked about her fight for women's equality, and the significant barriers that were broken by Helen's "firsts" as a female journalist.

Even some of the people and organizations that had issued harsh words when Helen's career unraveled had softened, only recalling her accomplishments. For instance, Helen's former colleagues with the White House Correspondents' Association said in a statement:

"Helen Thomas was a trailblazer in journalism and in the White House press corps, covering presidents from John F. Kennedy through Barack Obama.

Starting with the Kennedy administration, she was the first woman to cover the president and not just the first lady.

At her urging in 1962, Kennedy said he would not attend the annual dinner of the White House Correspondents' Association unless it was opened to women for the first time. It was.

And in 1975–76, she served as the first woman president of the association.

Women and men who've followed in the press corps all owe a debt of gratitude for the work Helen did and the doors she opened. All of our journalism is the better for it."

And President Barack Obama said:

"Helen was a true pioneer, opening doors and breaking down barriers for generations of women in journalism. She never failed to keep presidents—myself included—on their toes."

I was glad Helen was getting the recognition she deserved. While she should have never uttered the hateful remarks that she made to the rabbi, those words did not diminish her years of accomplishments.

Helen's body was cremated, and memorial services were planned in the Detroit area, and in Washington DC in the following months. There were three in all.

Memorial Services

Helen's family still primarily resided in the Detroit area, so they held the first memorial service on August 15 at St. George Antiochian Orthodox Church in Troy, Michigan, a suburb of Detroit. It came as a surprise to me that the service was held in a church since Helen repeatedly said she did not believe in organized religion, but since funerals are planned by the living, I thought it was okay.

I flew to Detroit the day before the service and stayed at my parents' house, not far from the church. My mom, dad, and I attended the memorial together. After all, my parents had known Helen well before I was born.

A coffee reception was held upon arrival, and we mingled with the other guests. The service featured one of Helen's Michigan-based nieces eulogizing her aunt, as well as singing and readings by her great-nieces and -nephews.

There was nothing mentioned about a "wake" after the memorial at the service, nor was there anything mentioned in the program. However, as my parents and I exited the church, it was apparent that all of the other guests were talking about the lunch they were headed for to celebrate Helen's life. Helen's great-niece from Washington asked if we could sit together at the lunch. While I stood there awkwardly, my mom finally said, "We weren't invited." I hugged Helen's great-niece, and my parents and I left for our own lunch. Apparently, all was not forgiven by some of Helen's family, and it was hurtful.

The second memorial in Helen's honor was a lunch given by Mama Ayesha's on August 25. Ayesha's nephew, who now runs the restaurant, asked me to speak at it. I was hesitant in light of how my parents and I were treated at the Detroit service, and I knew Helen's Washington-based family would be in attendance.

However, I was persuaded to speak by reassurances that many of my friends would be at the luncheon, as well as Helen's family. In the end, I was glad I had the opportunity to pay tribute to one of my closest, oldest friends.

About 40–50 people came to Ayesha's for the memorial lunch. Course after course of delicious food was served, and an exhibit was set up in the location that once was Helen's table at the restaurant. The display featured a collage of photos of Helen throughout her lifetime, including a framed photograph of Helen with Mama Ayesha.

My speech went well, and others offered their memories of the late White House correspondent. I wore a leopard print sweater since Helen loved anything with a leopard print. All in all, it was a nice tribute to Helen, and I thought she would have been pleased that everyone was eating at "her" restaurant while saluting her life.

The final memorial service was held on October 5 at the National Press Club. Helen's close friend Maggie Kilgore, who had helped Helen with one of her books, came for the event from California, and stayed with me.

Hundreds of people were seated in the ballroom to honor Helen. The irony did not escape me as I looked up at the balcony on both sides of the room, that it was Helen who had made it possible for female journalists to cover events at the NPC from where we were seated, rather than from the balcony area, and it was Helen who was the first female officer of this prestigious club.

Guests heard from Helen's friends, including ABC's Sam Donaldson, *PBS NewsHour*'s Judy Woodruff, *USA Today*'s Susan Page, actress Diane Ladd, and Dear Abby's daughter, Jeanne Phillips (who has taken over her mother's advice column). Some of the speeches were funny, and some were more sentimental.

It was a nice way to say goodbye to a great journalist, and a good friend.

Afterword

Many years have elapsed since Helen's passing, and these years have given me time to reflect. I have concluded that I cherish my *Life with Helen*.

Helen's inappropriate, hateful remarks to Rabbi Nesenoff tarnished Helen's career and soiled her place in history. The words should never have been uttered. Hateful speech has no place in civil society. But I believe Helen was heartbroken the last three years of her life for having made those comments, and her words when she was aged, sick, and frail do not take away her many trailblazing accomplishments. Nor do they take away the many kindnesses Helen showered on so many people, including me.

So, I choose to dwell on the good times. I remember the time one late evening when I had just moved out of Helen's place into my own condo in the same building. I was talking on the phone with a friend in New York when I suddenly saw two mice flatten their bodies and come into my home under the door from the hallway. I began screaming, and I yelled to the point that my friend on the other end of the phone asked if she should call 911. I explained that mice were in my home and asked what I should do. My friend said, "Call Helen!"

I immediately hung up the phone and dialed Helen's number. When I conveyed what was happening, Helen reticently asked, "Did you want me to come up to your place?" I replied, "Yes! And please hurry!" Soon thereafter, Helen arrived at my door holding a broom and an umbrella. When I asked what the items were for, she said, "These are my weapons!" We stood in my living room, looking around. All of a sudden, one of the mice jetted across the room. We both screamed and jumped onto the sofa. Helen then declared, "We can't handle these mice by ourselves. Get something to sleep in, and you will stay at my house tonight. We can call an exterminator in the morning." I stayed at Helen's for a couple of days until the exterminator told me both mice had been captured.

I also fondly recall a party Helen took me to at the White House during the Clinton years. The South Lawn had been transformed into a carnival, complete with hot dog and cotton candy trucks. There also were rides. Helen took one look around and determined we would not be taking part in any of the "dangerous" rides. Then she spotted one that she thought might be acceptable. As we approached the merry-go-round, Helen stated, "We won't be going on those animals that go up and down, but we can ride on one of the stationary benches." Helen giggled, the entire time watching and marveling at the horses we weren't allowed to ride.

Helen was always there for me, too. Like the time I

broke my ankle, and the doctor ordered an MRI. The MRI technology was new at the time, so I was afraid, not knowing what to expect. Helen not only came to the hospital with me, but she insisted on sitting in a chair where I could see her while I had the MRI.

Helen and I frequently shopped for clothes together. She liked to go to Lord + Taylor, and after we finished shopping, she also liked to have lunch at the restaurant in the store. The restaurant had terrible food—by Helen's own admission. But she liked one of the waitresses who had worked there for years and years. We repeatedly discussed the fact that we didn't know who was older: the waitress or the rest of the patrons who made the place resemble a nursing home. And Helen loved the hot fudge sundaes.

Then there were Helen's many encounters with cats and dogs—animals she loathed. One time, when I was going to drive back to Michigan after my summer internship was over, I planned to have my grandmother, Me-mama, fly to Washington to accompany me on the ten-hour journey. Instead, Helen suggested she ride with me so she could see her family in the Detroit area.

We set out on the lengthy trip and arrived at my parents' house. Our two families planned to have dinner together that evening. I called my parents at work to let them know we were there, and I left Helen sitting in a chair in the family room near a phone to call her family. I began unloading things from my car, running up and down the stairs to my bedroom.

While I was upstairs, I heard Helen shrieking. I couldn't imagine what was happening, so I bolted down the stairs. Helen was standing in the corner, behind the chair I left her in. And there was our Siamese cat proudly sitting in front of Helen, just staring at her. I scooped up the cat, and Helen said with a giggle, "She's after me!"

On another occasion when I lived with Helen, my parents came for a visit. They knew a couple who lived in Georgetown, and they invited all of us to have brunch at their home. As we got out of the car when we arrived, the couple opened the door and stepped outside to greet us. A dog bounded out the door, and Helen exclaimed, "Oh, they have a dog!" Suddenly, another dog came from the open door, causing Helen to say in a loud voice, "Ohhh! They have *two* dogs!" We went into the house, and the couple escorted our group to the back patio for hors d'oeuvres and drinks. It was a lovely day, but not so much for Helen when four dogs formed a semi-circle around her feet. Helen jumped out of her chair and, mustering her calmest voice, said, "I see you have four dogs!" Not realizing Helen was afraid, the couple proceeded to talk about how they thought of the dogs as their later-in-life children. Helen simply said, "I see," and moved her chair away from the animals.

One time, I was rewarded by Helen for my love of cats. President Bill Clinton and his family had a cat, Socks, who lived at the White House with them. Helen occasionally spotted Socks, and she grumbled to me about why they had to have a cat. The president was not aware of how Helen felt about pets, and on her birthday one year, he gave her a pin of Socks playing the saxophone, an instrument the president played himself. Helen accepted the pin, thanking President Clinton for the kind gift. Then she called me to ask me to meet her for dinner, telling me she had something special for me. That evening, Helen presented me with the Socks pin, and I still have it.

The Socks pin (almost) came in handy the following March. My dad came to town to attend the white-tie Gridiron dinner as one of Helen's guests. As I was getting ready for the dinner, there was a knock on my bedroom door. I told my dad I was dressed, and to come in. My dad said, "You don't happen to have a white tie laying around somewhere, do you?" I spun around from the mirror where I was putting on my makeup and said, "What do you mean? I hope you didn't forget your white tie! We have to meet Helen in the lobby in five minutes!" To clarify the obvious: my dad had not brought a white tie with him. But I had an idea. I took the Socks pin out of my jewelry box and suggested he wear it in place of the missing tie. I thought it was better than nothing, and because President Clinton was speaking at the dinner, I thought it was the perfect substitute for the tie.

An argument ensued, and my dad refused to wear the Socks pin. We were still arguing as we got off the elevator to meet Helen to go to the dinner, and I was still holding the pin. We both spoke to Helen at once, trying to make our cases for wearing the pin versus not wearing it. Helen raised her voice slightly to be heard above our arguing. She told us the concierge at the venue for the dinner always had extra white ties, but she looked at my father and added, "I *do* think the pin would add something to your outfit, though!"

So, I remember Helen's heart. Her laughter. Her fun side.

Helen always tried to do her best, but like all of us, she fell short on occasion. She always inspired me to be my best, but at times, I fall short, too. All humans are flawed, and Helen was no exception.

In the current climate in our country and throughout the world, I believe Helen would have thought twice about her choice of words to the rabbi. She would have been appalled at the tone of the rhetoric from some of our elected officials, and she would have condemned the violence that is increasingly common in the world, including the abhorrent shootings and bombings of churches, synagogues, and mosques. She was in favor of a peace-filled, joyful world for all of humankind. She constantly used to say, "Let's try to reject war and give peace a chance."

I also think Helen would be horrified by the increasingly frequent attacks on the media, both verbal and physical. There has never been a greater champion of a free press than Helen Thomas. She used to say there was a reason why the First Amendment is first in the Bill of Rights. It's "because all of our individual freedoms flow from the First Amendment, and without a free press, there can be no democracy."

There were so many good times with this legend, and I am grateful to her for teaching me so much about journalism, politics, and life, in general. When I stopped being Helen's agent, I never stopped being her friend.

I miss my friend. I still reach for the phone to call Helen when I have good news, bad news, or no news at all—just longing to hear her voice.

Photos

All photos from author's personal collection.

Helen and her siblings

Me-mama's nursing school graduation

Me-mama and Isabelle "Issy" Thomas – Lifelong best
friends

Helen and Diane – After Diane's high school graduation

Helen and Diane

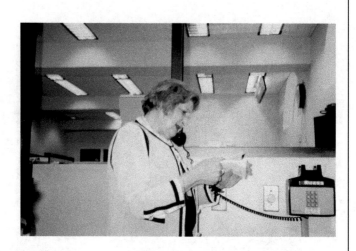

Helen at work in the UPI booth at the White House

The Ladies: (back row) Gloria, Helen, Dorothy O
(front) Fran

Dorothy Newman

Helen and Fran Lewine on the job with JFK

Sue, Fran, Dorothy O., Helen, Gloria – New Year's Eve
pajama party

Helen and Dorothy Newman

Helen's white condo

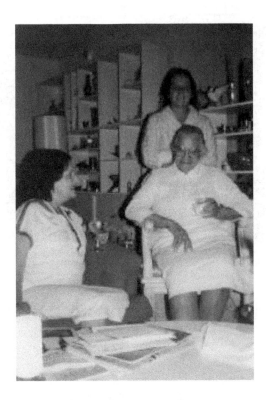

Helen, her housekeeper Nellie, Diane

Helen and Mama Ayesha

Helen and Diane with Jimmy and Rosalynn Carter in
White House Briefing Room

Paul Nine (Diane's father), Helen, Dear Abby, Sue Nine
(Diane's mother)–Before Gridiron Dinner

Helen and Diane at White House Correspondent's
Dinner

Diane, Bill and Hillary Clinton, Helen at White House
Christmas Party

Helen signing books

In loving memory

Helen Amelia Thomas

AUGUST 4, 1920 - JULY 20, 2013

Program from memorial service held in Troy, MI

Diane speaking at memorial service at Mama Ayesha's

About the Author

Diane S. Nine is the president of Nine Speakers, Inc., a full-service entertainment agency representing people across the world in a number of areas including the literary, lecture, theatrical, film, and television arenas. Diane is a graduate of Cranbrook Schools, Denison University, and George Washington University's Law School. She knew Helen Thomas her entire life and was Helen's agent from 1988 through 2010.

Printed in the USA
CPSIA information can be obtained
at www.ICGtesting.com
LVHW021150230823
756049LV00012B/95/J